Big Chinese Workbook for Little Hands

小手写中文

Written by Yang Yang

Consulting editors: Han Xu, Qin Chen, Claire Wang, Yi Chen, Ke Peng

这是＿＿＿＿＿＿的书。

This book belongs to:

＿＿＿＿＿＿＿＿＿＿＿＿

ISBN: 978-1539101840

Dear Parents,

Big Chinese workbook for Little Hands is a series of Chinese workbooks specifically designed for children living in English speaking countries and/or regions. Since its first publication in April of 2016, this workbook has soon become a bestseller in Children's Chinese Language Books across the US.

Upon completion of Level 1, your child should be able to:

- Understand the basic structures of Chinese characters.
- Identify and write 22 most commonly used radicals.
- Understand and adapt to the correct stroke order when writing Chinese characters.
- Talk briefly about time, weather, and seasons.
- Understand and tell the opposite of 26 pairs of antonyms.
- Ask and answer the WH questions (Who, Which, What, When, Where, Why, or How.)
- Read up to 250 new characters and write 100 of them (including 10 more sight words, in addition to the ones learned in Level K).

Total vocabulary for Level K+ Level 1
reading: 550   writing: 165

Recommended usage: 2-4 pages at a time, two times a week. Read, review, and rewrite by memory the old characters before moving on to new exercises.

Helpful hint: Don't forget to photocopy the grid at the back of this book for more writing practice!

养成这样的习惯，学习效果会更好：

1. 每次做练习之前，都大声朗读上一次做过的部分，再默写一次写过的字。
2. 学写一个生字的时候，（在老师或家长的指导下）边写边说出笔画的名称。
比如写"口"的时候，就边写边说竖、横折、横。
3. 每个生字描写两遍、抄写一遍以后，就遮住写过的字，试着自己默写（最后两格）。
4. 鼓励孩子用每个生字组词或造句。

祝您的孩子中文进步！

FAQs

汉字是象形文字吗？
Are Chinese characters pictographic?

　　汉字有六种构字法，象形、指事、会意、形声、转注、假借，合称为 "六书"，其中象形字只占很少的一部分，而 80%以上的汉字都是形声字，形声字通常由一个形旁和一个声旁组成。

Chinese characters are formed in six different ways. Only a very small set of Chinese characters are pictographic. The vast majority (over 80%) are phono-semantic compounds, which are usually composed of a semantic radical and a phonetic component.

什么是部首？为什么要学部首？
What is a radical? Why is it important to learn radicals?

　　部首是一些汉字共同的偏旁，是字典里分类汉字的基准。所有汉字都归类在某一个部首之下。部首通常表义，但也可能表音, 或是一些汉字共有的部件, 甚至只是一个笔画。而最常用的表义部首，每个都可以产生几百字。因此，学会了部首，就如同掌握了中文的拼写规则。

A radical 部首 (literally meaning "section header") is a graphical component of a Chinese character under which the character is listed in a dictionary. In most cases, it is a semantic indicator that carries meaning. In other cases, it can be a phonetic component, a portion shared by a group of characters, or simply a stroke.

In other words, 部首 is like a family name，and every Chinese character has a family name. In English, kids learn the rules of spelling and pronunciation through phonics. For example, "bat"，"hat"，"pat"，and "mat" belong to the "-at" family, and "-at" is like their family name. In Chinese, 亻 (meaning people) is like the family name of the 亻 family where 你 (you)，他 (he) and 休 (rest) belong. The most productive radicals can each generate hundreds of characters. Since radicals usually come from the very basic characters, they are simple in shape and easy to understand. Once a child knows the radicals, he/she will understand the rules of Chinese "spelling".

In this book, we only talk about the radicals that carry meaning, the semantic radicals.

 # Contents

字形结构
Character Structures

Some characters only have 1 part and cannot be separated.
They are called Single-Component Characters.

Color each character with <u>one</u> color.

rén
people

tiān
sky

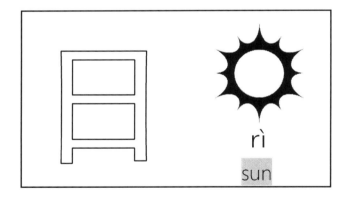

rì
sun

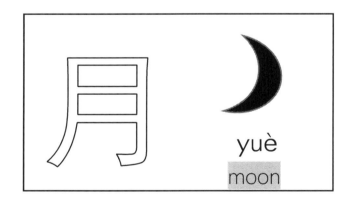

yuè
moon

nǚ
female

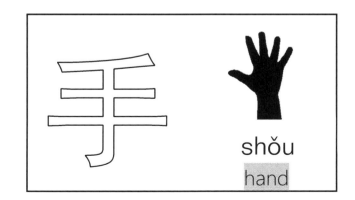

shǒu
hand

Color more Single-Component Characters.

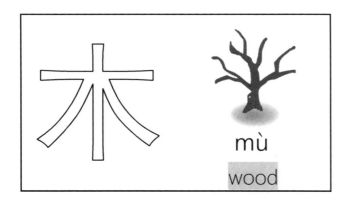

mù

wood

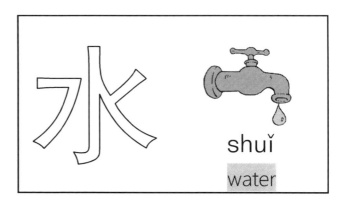

shuǐ

water

huǒ

fire

tǔ

earth, soil

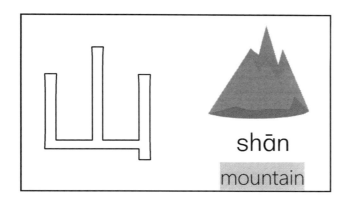

shān

mountain

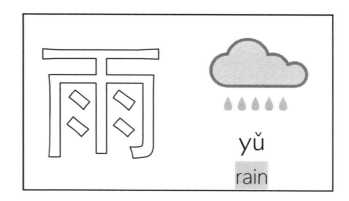

yǔ

rain

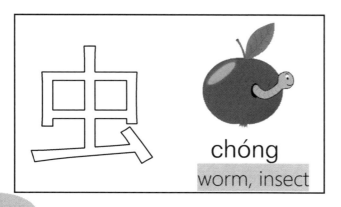

chóng

worm, insect

mǐ

rice

Many characters have 2 parts.
Color each character with 2 colors (one color for each part). Look at the blocks for clue.

好

hǎo
good

妈

mā
mom

你

nǐ
you

他

tā
he, him

朋

péngyou
朋友
friends

和

hé wǒ
你和我
you and me

7

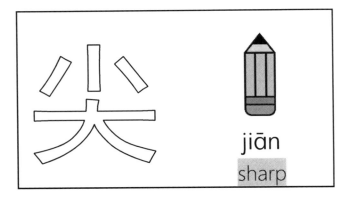

尖
jiān
sharp

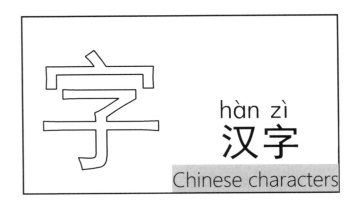

字
hàn zì
汉字
Chinese characters

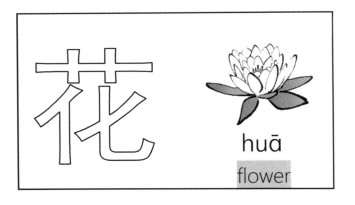

花
huā
flower

笑
xiào
smile

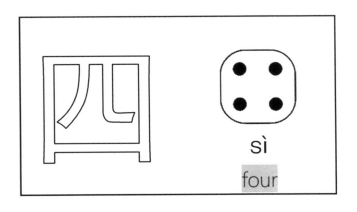

四
sì
four

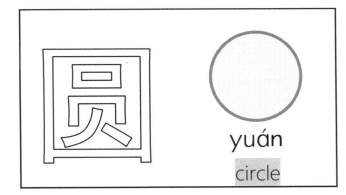

圆
yuán
circle

爬 pá
crawl, climb

过 guò
pass, cross

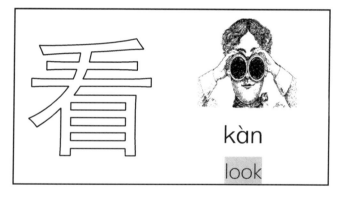

看 kàn
look

尾 wěi ba
尾巴
tail

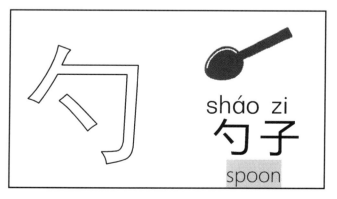

勺 sháo zi
勺子
spoon

可 kě yǐ
可以
can, may

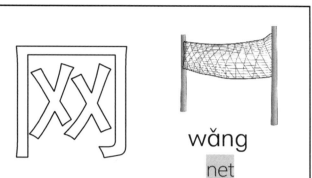

wǎng

net

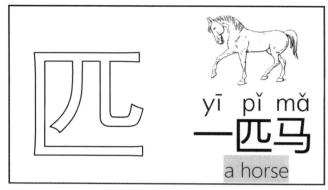

yī pǐ mǎ
一匹马

a horse

Some characters have 3 parts.
Color them with 3 colors (one color for each part).

shù

tree

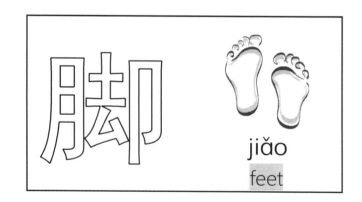

jiǎo

feet

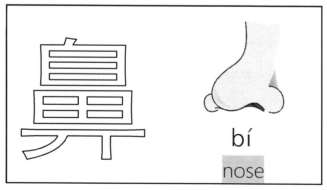

bí

nose

chá

tea

Characters that have two or more parts are called Multi-component characters. Most of these characters have a part that tells a clue of its meaning, and it's called a semantic radical.

Circle 女 (female) in these characters.

mā — 妈 — mom

jiě — 姐 — older sister

tā — 她 — she

Circle 犭 (animals that look like dogs) in these characters.

māo — 猫 — cat

gǒu — 狗 — dog

zhū — 猪 — pig

女 and 犭 are the semantic radical in these characters.

A semantic radical may appear at any position in a character. Its shape may be changed so to better fit into a block.

1. 旁^{páng} On the side （Example: 单^{dān} 人旁）

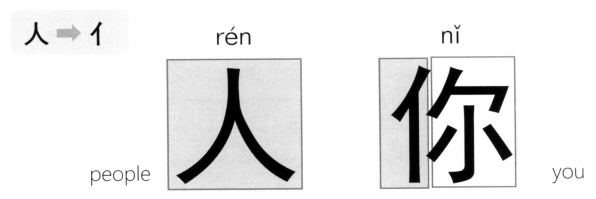

2. 头^{tóu} On the top （Example: 雨字^{zì}头）

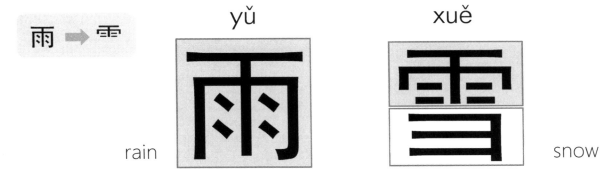

3. 底^{dǐ} On the bottom （Example: 土^{tǔ}字底）

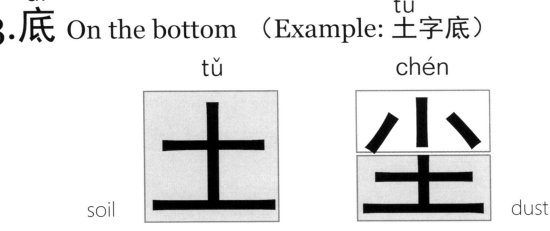

4. Other positions

Can you find the semantic radical in 粥，看，and 爬?
Color in their blocks.

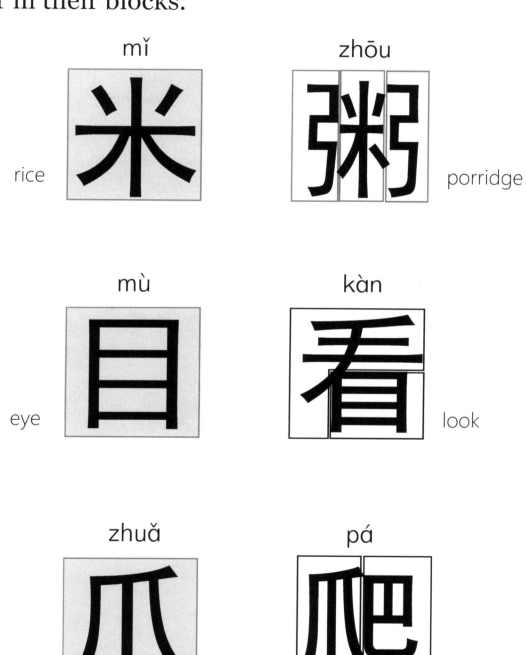

mǐ

rice

zhōu

porridge

mù

eye

kàn

look

zhuǎ

claw

pá

crawl

部首练习
Semantic Radicals

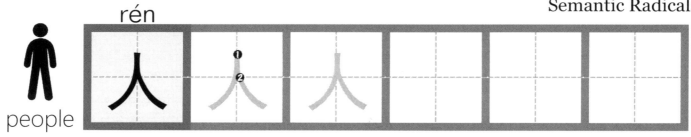

rén

人

people

Complete the words with 人.

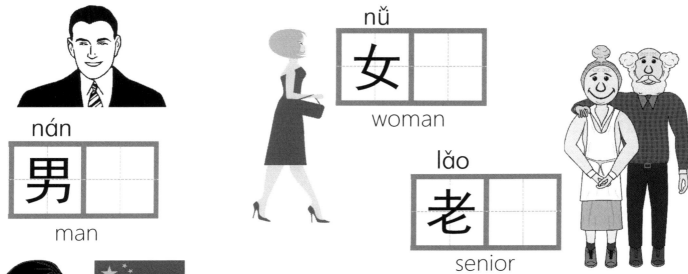

nán

男 ☐

man

nǚ

女 ☐

woman

lǎo

老 ☐

senior

zhōng guó

中 国 ☐

Chinese (people)

měi

美 国 ☐

American (people)

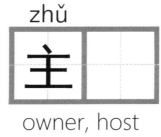

zhǔ

主 ☐

owner, host

kè

客 ☐

guest

人字头 (人 tóu on the top)

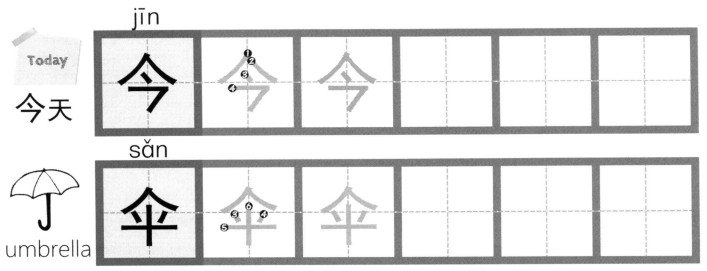

jīn
今

今天

sǎn
伞

umbrella

Find and trace 人 in these characters.

quán bān
全班
whole class

hé chàng
合唱
together sing

guān zhòng
观众
audience

dǎ
打伞
hold up an umbrella

jīn yú huì yóu yǒng
金鱼会游泳
gold fish can swim

16

dān
单人旁 (人 on the side) 人 ➡ 亻

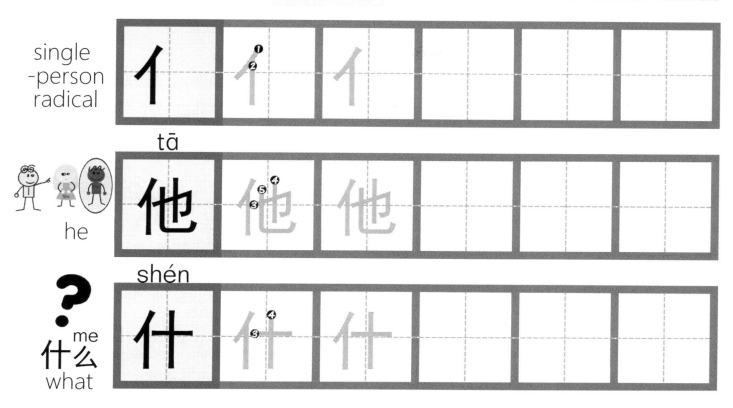

single -person radical
亻

tā
他
he

shén
什
什么
me
what

What is he/ she doing? Find and trace 亻.

zài   zuò
他在做什么？
do
他在休息。
rest
xi

xiū
休

她在做什么？
zuò   yè
她在做作业。
homework

17

men

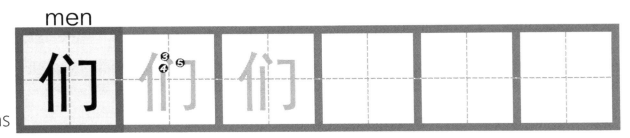

Use 们 to extend the words.

wǒ
我 ➡ 我 们
I   we

你 ➡ 你 ☐
you   you (plural)

他 ➡ 他 ☐
he   they

她 ➡ 她 ☐
she   they (all female)

tā
它 ➡ 它 ☐
it   they (animals)

18

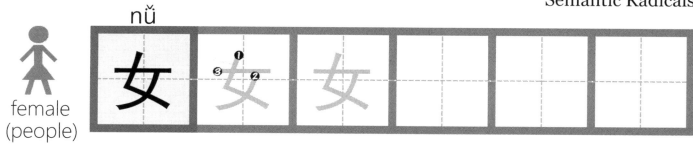

nǚ

女 女 女

female
(people)

Complete the words with 女.

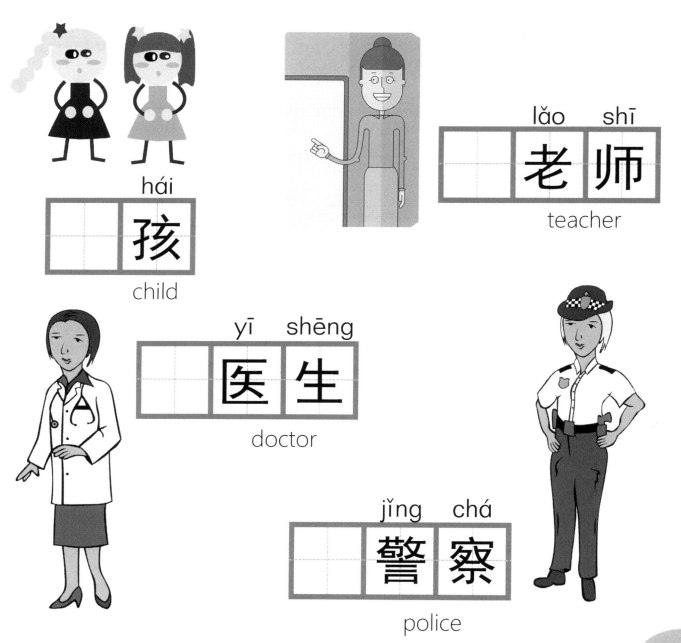

lǎo shī

老 师

teacher

hái

孩

child

yī shēng

医 生

doctor

jǐng chá

警 察

police

女字旁 (女 on the side)／女字底 (女 on the bottom)

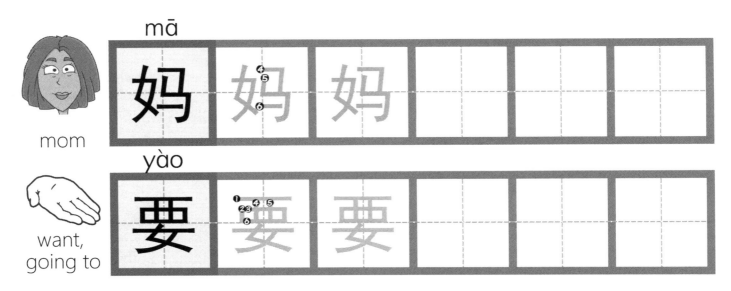

mā
妈 妈 妈
mom

yào
要 要 要
want, going to

Find and trace 女 in these words.

jiě
姐姐
older sister

mèi
妹妹
younger sister

ā yí
阿姨
aunt, mom's sister

gū
姑姑
aunt, dad's sister

wài pó
外婆
grandma, mom's mom

nǎi
奶奶
grandma, dad's mom

20

父/父字头

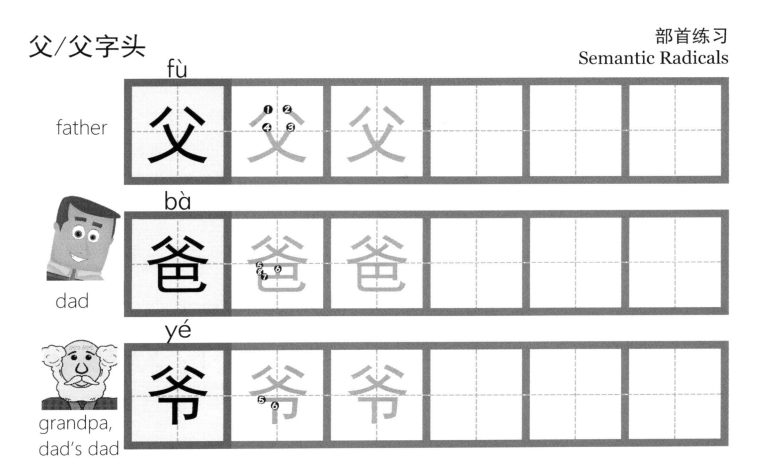

father — fù 父 父 父

dad — bà 爸 爸 爸

grandpa, dad's dad — yé 爷 爷 爷

Look at the pictures and fill in the blanks.

爷爷　奶奶

爸爸

wài gōng

外公　外婆

妈妈

爸爸 de 的 妈妈 shì 是 __奶奶__ ，妈妈的_____是外婆。

('s) (is)

爸爸的爸爸是_____，妈妈的_____是外公。

21

男 or 女？ Color the cards. Use blue for male and pink for female.

nán
男
Male

女
Female

爸爸	妈妈	爷爷	奶奶

外公	外婆	哥哥	姐姐

弟弟	妹妹	姑姑	阿姨

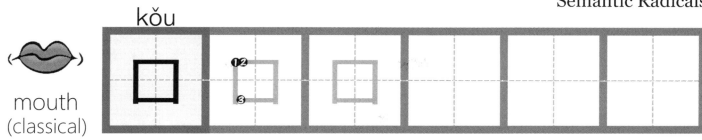

kǒu

mouth
(classical)

Complete the words with 口.

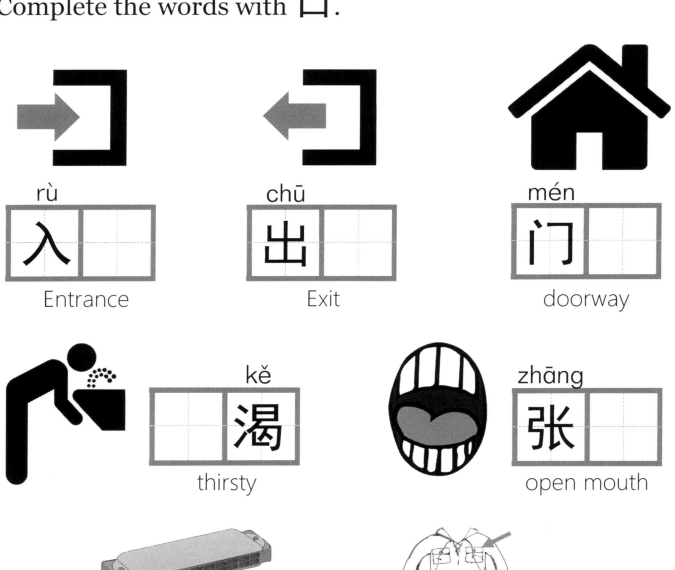

rù

入

Entrance

chū

出

Exit

mén

门

doorway

kě

渴

thirsty

zhāng

张

open mouth

qín

琴

harmonica

dài

袋

pocket

Find and trace 口 in these characters.

yòu
右
right

hòu
后
back, behind

哥哥

kū
哭
cry

Get out of the giant's mouth!

出口

入口

24

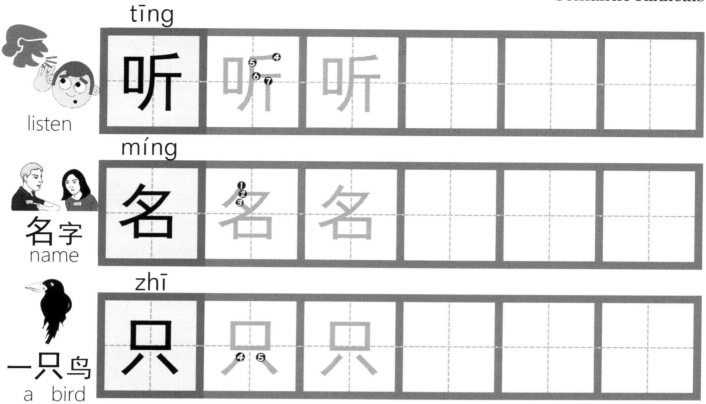

tīng
听 听 听

listen

míng
名 名 名

名字
name

zhī
只 只 只

一只鸟
a bird

Find and trace 口 in these characters.

chī fàn
吃饭
eat rice/ meal

hē
喝水

shé tou
舌头

chuī pào
吹泡泡

blow bubbles

hào
三月五号

March
5

zuǐ ba
嘴巴

mouth

Read and match the animals with the sounds they make.

xiǎo māo jiào   miāo
小猫叫 喵喵
little cat call (say) meow-meow

qīng wā   guā
青蛙叫 呱呱
frog   ribbit-ribbit

jī   jī
小鸡叫 叽叽
chicken   cluck-cluck

yā   gā
小鸭叫 嘎嘎
duck   quack-quack

yáng   miē
小羊叫 咩咩
sheep   baa-baa

niú   mōu
小牛叫 哞哞
cow   moo-moo

Read and sing.

Old McDonald Had a Farm

wáng lǎo xiānsheng yǒu kuài dì
王 老 先 生 有 块 地，
old   Mr. Wang   land

yī yā   yōu
咿呀咿呀呦，

lǐ yǎng
他在地里 养 小鸡，咿呀咿呀呦，
raise

jī
叽叽叽， 叽叽叽，

叽叽叽叽叽叽叽，

王老先生有块地，咿呀咿呀呦。

Substitute the underlined words and sing more!

gā
小鸭　嘎嘎

miē
小羊　咩咩

mōu
小牛　哞哞

27

王老先生有块地

Traditional

王 老 先 生　　有 块 地，　　咿 呀 咿 呀　　呦

他 在 地 里　　养 小 鸡，　　咿 呀 咿 呀　　呦

叽 叽 叽　　叽 叽 叽　　叽 叽 叽 叽　　叽 叽 叽

王 老 先 生　　有 块 地，　　咿 呀 咿 呀　　呦

shǒu

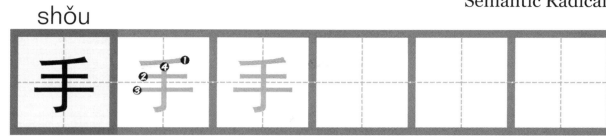

hand

Complete the words with 手.

biǎo

表

watch

jī

机

cell phone

gōng

工

hand craft

tào

套

gloves, mittens

wò

握

shake hands

29

Find the hidden 手 in these characters. Some of them may have slight changes.

quán tou
拳头

fist

ná
拿

take, hold

pān yán
攀岩

climb rock

bài nián
拜年

wish Happy New Year

Fill in the blanks with
zuǒ
左手 or 右手 .
left

yòng
我用 [   ] 刷牙。
use   shuā yá
             brush teeth

我用 [   ] 吃饭。

我用 [   ] 写字。
              xiě zì
              write

我用 [   ] 拍球。
              pāi qiú
              bounce a ball

30

tí
提手旁 手 ➡ 扌

hand radical

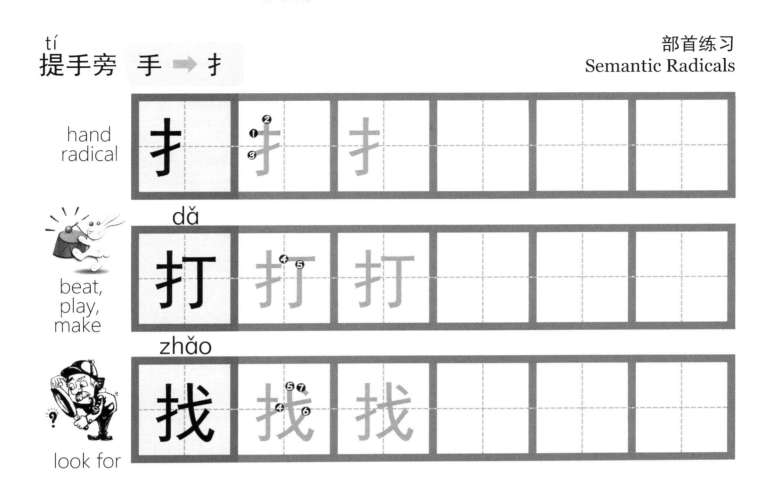

dǎ
打
beat, play, make

zhǎo
找
look for

Find and trace 扌 in these characters.

sǎo dì
扫地
sweep floor

tuō
拖地
mop

zhǎo
找朋友

pāi qiú
拍球

rēng
扔球
throw

jiē
接球
catch

31

Read and circle the characters that have 扌. Then complete the characters in the boxes.

 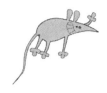 

小花猫，找朋友，
huā

找到一只小老鼠。
dào   lǎo shǔ
find

小老鼠，摇摇头：
yáo
shake

"我不是你的好朋友。"
bú

| 戈 | 朋 | 友 |

| 匋 | 匋 | 头 |

小花猫，往前走，
wǎng qián zǒu
forward walk

找到一条大黑狗，
tiáo   hēi gǒu

握握手，扭一扭，
wò   niǔ
twist, waggle

一起 来玩 拍皮球。
qǐ lái wán   pí
together come play rubber ball

| 屋 | 屋 | 手 |

| 丑 | 一 | 丑 |

| 白 | 皮 | 球 |

We do many things with our hands. Read the words and trace the 扌.

diào
手机掉了
drop

jiǎn qǐ lái
捡起来
pick up

tuī mén
推门
push

lā chē
拉车
pull wagon (vehicle)

zhuā
抓头
scratch

mō xiàng
摸象
touch, elephant feel

wā tǔ
挖土
dig

káng
扛起来
carry on shoulder

tái
抬 zhuō zi
桌子
lift   table

bān
搬 jiā
家
move

àn ménlíng
按 门铃
press doorbell

yōng bào
拥抱
hug

打球

zhuō
捉 老鼠
capture

bá
拔河
pull river
(tug of war)

shuāi dǎo
摔倒
fall down

Do you help your family with housework? Circle the chores that you do at home, and underline the characters with 扌.

cā zhuō
擦桌子
wipe

扫地

拖地

lā jī
扔垃圾
trash

bá cǎo
拔草
pull out weed

shù yè
扫树叶
leaf

bǎi cān jù
摆餐具
put, set tableware

guà yī fu
挂衣服
hang up   clothes

35

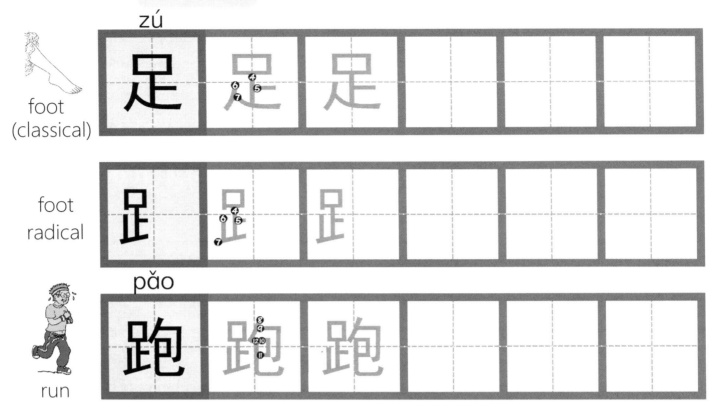

zú

足　足　足

foot (classical)

foot radical

𧾷　𧾷　𧾷

pǎo

跑　跑　跑

run

Find and trace 𧾷 in these characters.

tiào shéng
跳 绳
jump rope

tī qiú
踢 球
kick

bèng chuáng
蹦 床
bounce bed (trampoline)

zǒu lù
走 路
walk (road)

cǎi kēng
踩 水坑
step in puddle

gēn lái
跟 我来
follow, with

Hand or foot?

Complete the characters with 扌 or 𤴓.

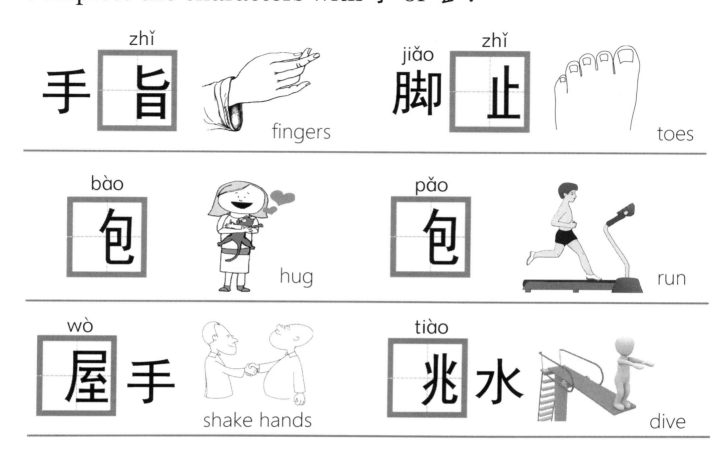

zhǐ		zhǐ
手 旨	jiǎo	脚 止
fingers		toes

bào — 包 — hug

pǎo — 包 — run

wò — 屋 手 — shake hands

tiào — 兆 水 — dive

Read this nursery rhyme and circle the words with 𤴓.

bái tù　　　yòu
小白兔，白又白，
white rabbit　　and

liǎng zhī ěr duo shù qǐ lái
两只耳朵 竖起来。
two　　ears standing upright

ài chī luó bo hé qīng cài
爱吃萝卜和青菜，
loves eating carrots and veggies

bèng　　tiào　　zhēn kě ài
蹦蹦跳跳真可爱。
really　cute

目/目字旁/目字底

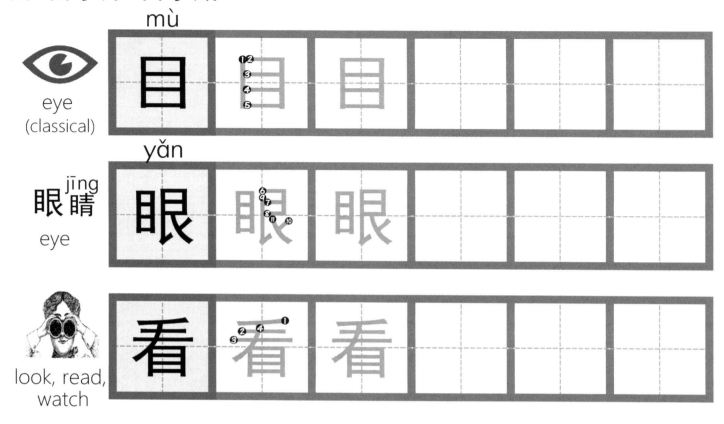

mù

目

eye
(classical)

yǎn

眼睛
jīng

眼

eye

看

look, read,
watch

Find and trace 目 in these characters.

kàn shū
看书
read a book

méi mao
眉毛
eyebrow

shuì jiào
睡觉
sleep

zhào xiàng
照相
take a photo

jìng
眼镜
glasses

zhēng kāi
睁开眼睛
open (eyes)

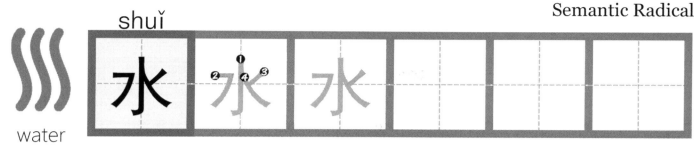

shuǐ

水 水 水

water

Complete the words with 水.

yǔ

雨 ☐

rain water

hǎi

海 ☐

sea water

kāi

开 ☐

boiling water

bēi

☐ 杯

water cup

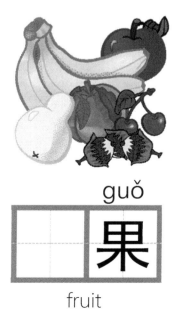

guǒ

☐ 果

fruit

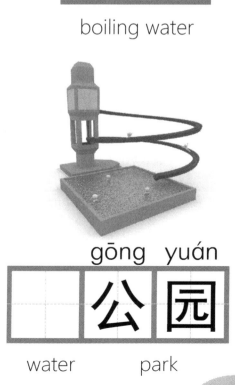

gōng yuán

☐ 公 园

water   park

39

What does a plant need to grow? Circle the words.

rì guāng
日光
sun light

月光

土

火

niú
牛奶

kōng qì
空气
air

miàn bāo
面包
bread

水

niǎo
小鸟

diǎn
三点水 水 ➡ 氵

water radical

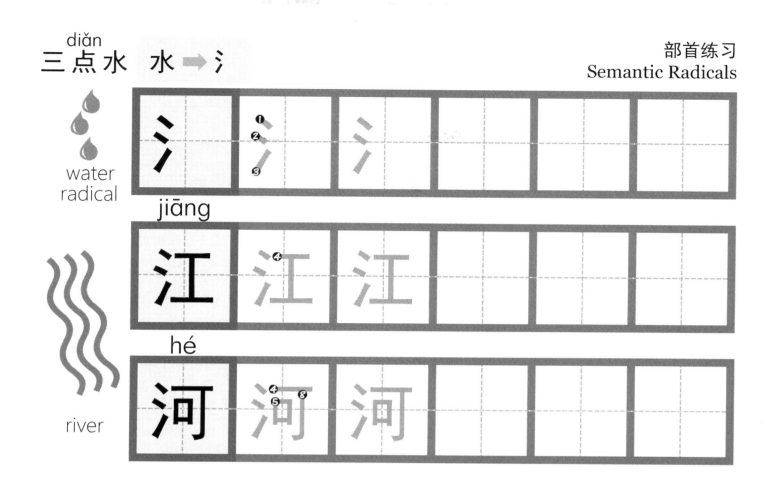

jiāng
江

hé
河

river

Can you find two hidden dragons on this map? They are the two longest rivers in China. Color 长江 蓝色 *lán sè* (blue), and 黄河 黄色 *huáng* (yellow).

黄河
Yellow River   #2 longest

长江
Yangtze River   #1 longest

Find and trace 氵 in these characters.

chū hàn
出汗
sweat

kě
渴了
thirsty

guǒ zhī
果汁
juice

yóu yǒng
游泳

xǐ zǎo
洗澡
take a bath

chuī pào
吹泡泡

Read and circle the characters that have 氵.

河里有小鸭，
lǐ — in
yā

小鸭爱洗澡。
ài — love

海里有大鱼，
yú — fish

大鱼吹泡泡。

两点水

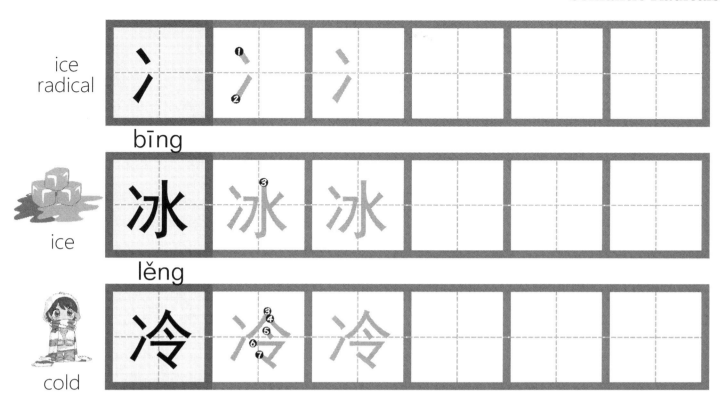

ice radical — 冫

bīng 冰 — ice

lěng 冷 — cold

Find and trace 冫 in these characters.

dòng
果**冻**
fruit jelly

qí lín
冰**淇淋**
ice cream

liáng kuài
凉**快**
cool

chōng
冲**水**
flush

What can we do with ice? Complete each word with 冰.

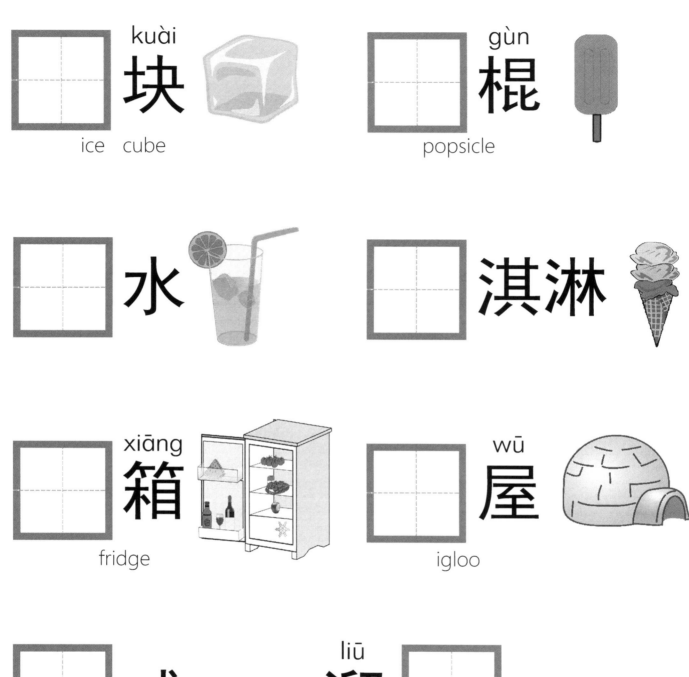

kuài
□ 块
ice cube

gùn
□ 棍
popsicle

□ 水

□ 淇淋

xiāng
□ 箱
fridge

wū
□ 屋
igloo

□ 球
ice hockey

liū
溜 □
skate

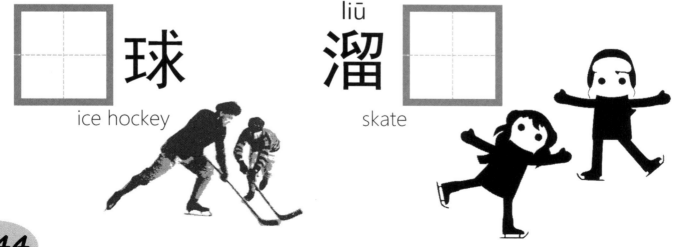

44

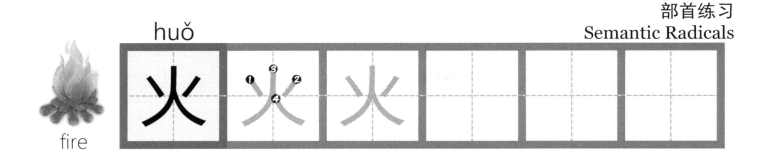

huǒ

fire

Complete the words with 火.

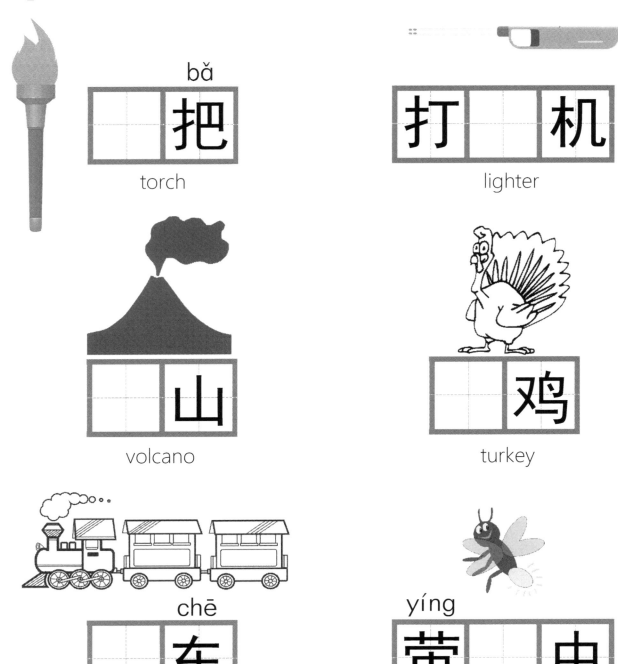

bǎ

把

torch

打　机

lighter

山

volcano

鸡

turkey

chē

车

train

yíng

萤　虫

firefly

火字旁/火字底

dēng

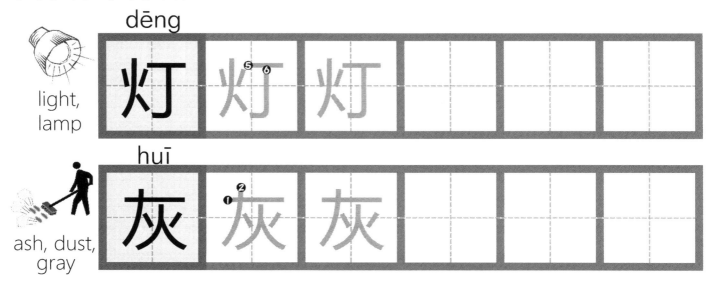

light, lamp

灯　灯　灯

huī

灰　灰　灰

ash, dust, gray

Find and trace 火 in these characters.

hóng lǜ

红绿灯

traffic light

kǎo miàn bāo

烤面包

toast　　bread

tàng

烫

hot (to the touch)

yān huā

烟花

fireworks

là zhú

蜡烛

candle

miè

灭火

extinguish

木/木字旁/木字底

mù

wood

木 木 木

bēi

cup

杯 杯 杯

duǒ

measure word for flowers

朵 朵 朵

Find and trace 木 in these characters.

hēi bǎn
黑板
blackboard

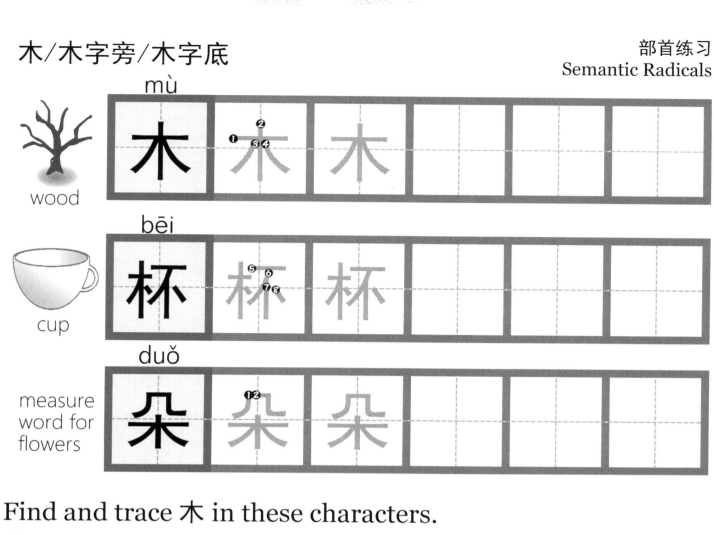

xué xiào
学校
school

sēn lín
森林
forest

两朵花
two   flowers

kē shù
一棵树
a   tree

棵：measure word for trees

47

What is made of wood? Find and circle the words that have 木 in them.

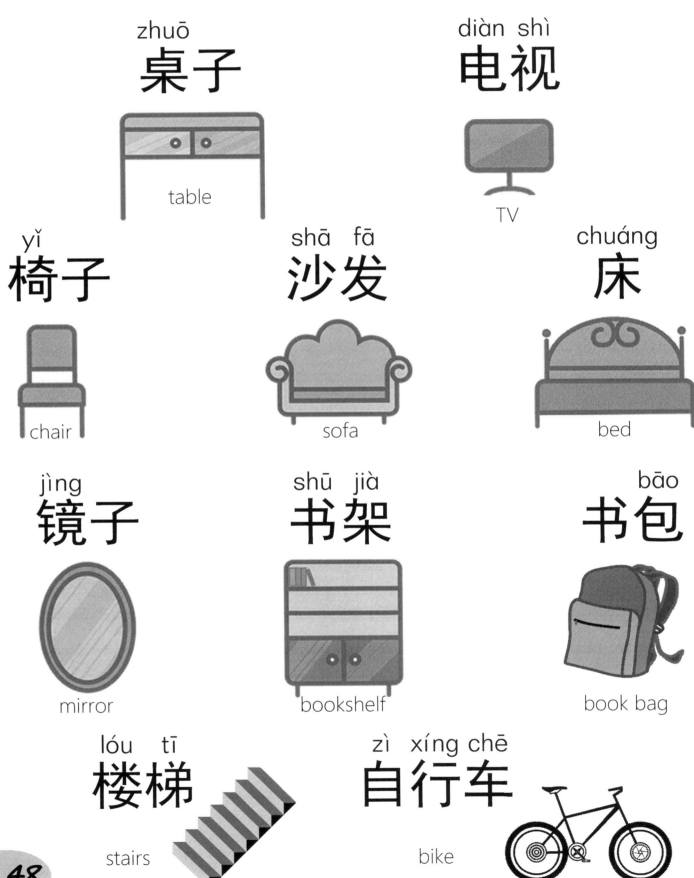

zhuō
桌子
table

diàn shì
电视
TV

yǐ
椅子
chair

shā fā
沙发
sofa

chuáng
床
bed

jìng
镜子
mirror

shū jià
书架
bookshelf

bāo
书包
book bag

lóu tī
楼梯
stairs

zì xíng chē
自行车
bike

土/提土^{tí}旁/土字底

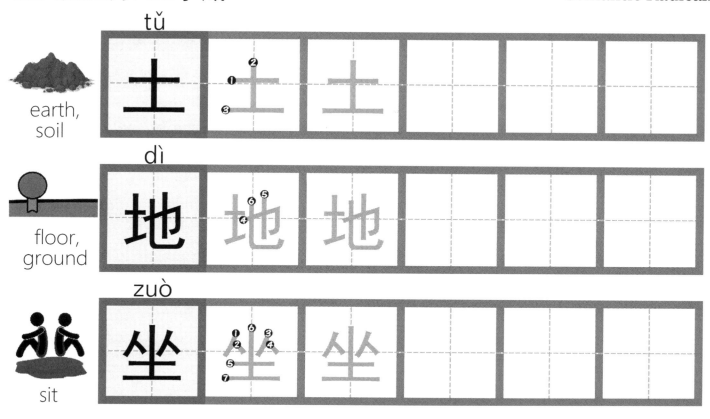

tǔ
土
earth, soil

dì
地
floor, ground

zuò
坐
sit

Find and trace 土 in these characters.

qiú
地球
earth

chén
灰尘
dust

duī xuě
堆雪人
stack (make) a snowman

lā jī
垃圾
trash

kēng
水坑
puddle

bǐng gān
两块饼干

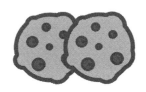

Metal, wood, water, fire, and earth are the five basic elements in nature. They create one another. Fill in the boxes with the five elements.

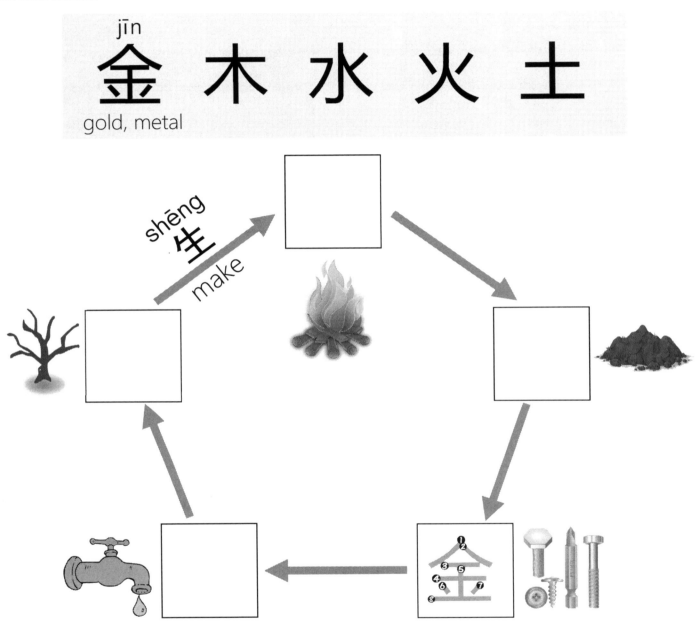

jīn
金 木 水 火 土

gold, metal

shēng
生
make

木生火 Wood feeds fire.

火生土 Fire creates earth (ash).

土生金 Earth bears metal.

金生水 Metal generates water.

水生木 Water nourishes wood.

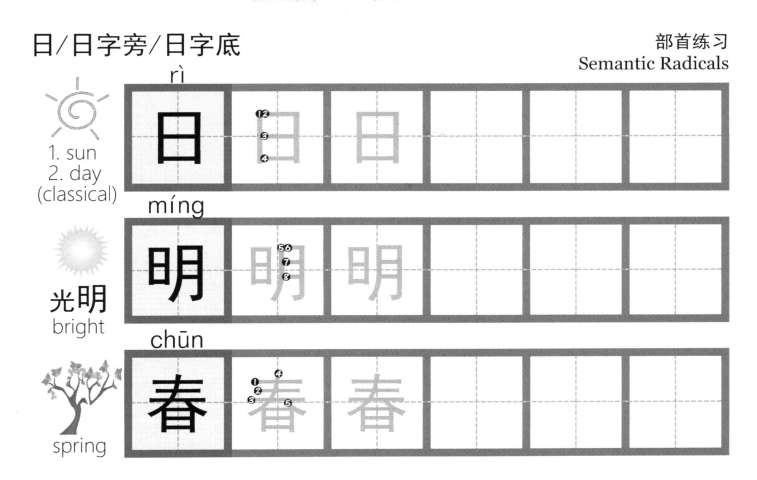

rì

日

1. sun
2. day (classical)

míng

明

光明
bright

chūn

春

spring

Find and trace 日 in these characters.

jié
春节

Spring Festival

wǎn
晚上好

good evening

ān
晚安

good night

zuó
昨天

Yesterday

明天

Tomorrow

qíng
晴天

sunny day

51

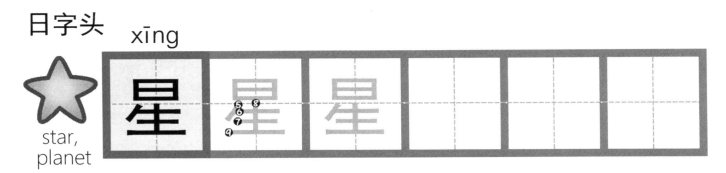

日字头　xīng

星　星　星

star, planet

Color the planets and say their names in Chinese.

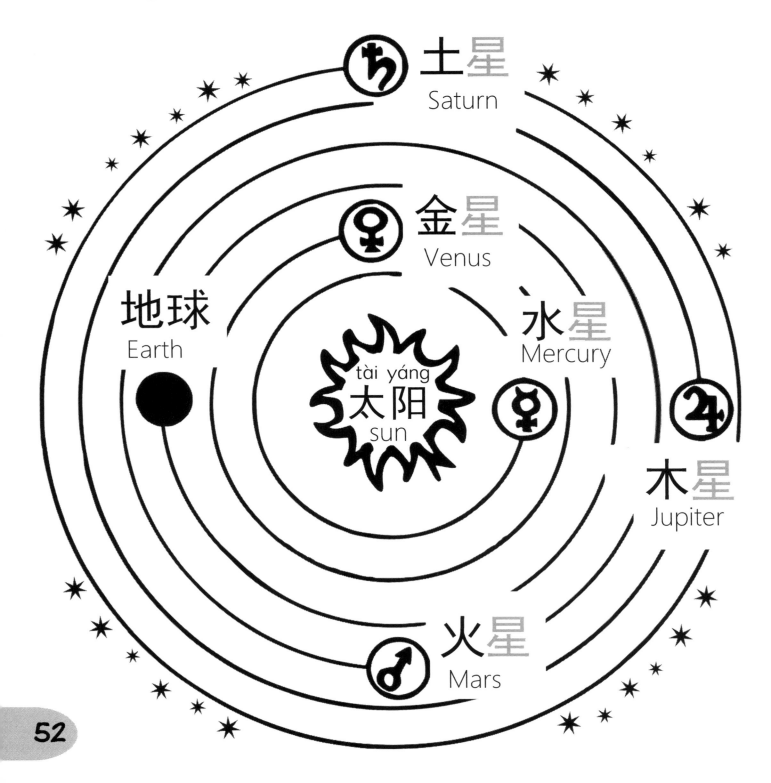

土星
Saturn

金星
Venus

地球
Earth

水星
Mercury

tài yáng
太阳
sun

木星
Jupiter

火星
Mars

雨/雨字头　雨 ➡ 雷

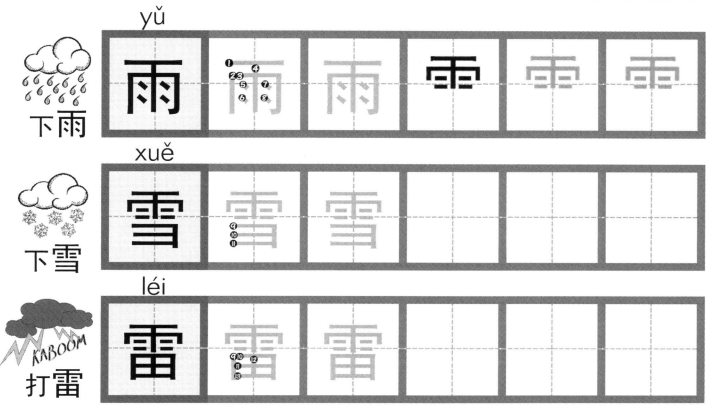

Fill in the boxes with 雨/雪.

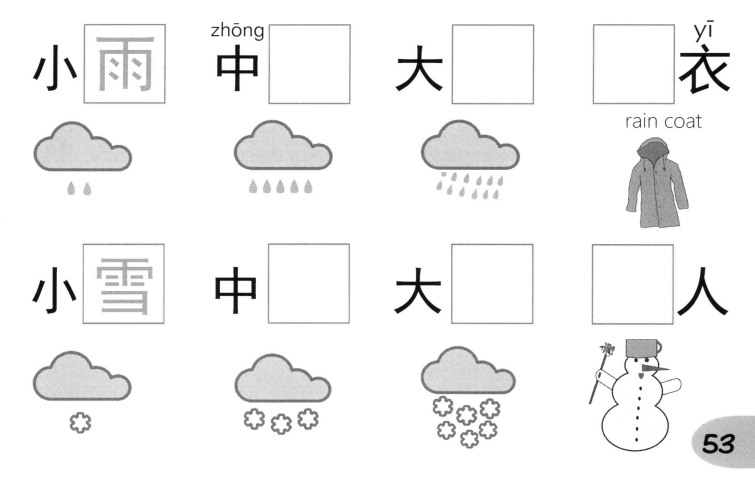

Hidden Character. Color the boxes by the code.

Characters with 雨/雨字头＝蓝色

人		雨			土	
火		雪	水			
雷						

雷	水	天			天		雨
		雨	手	雪	足	雪	
		女				父	
		雪				雨	水
木		木				木	口
		雪				雷	
		日					
		雷					
		土					
		雨					

54

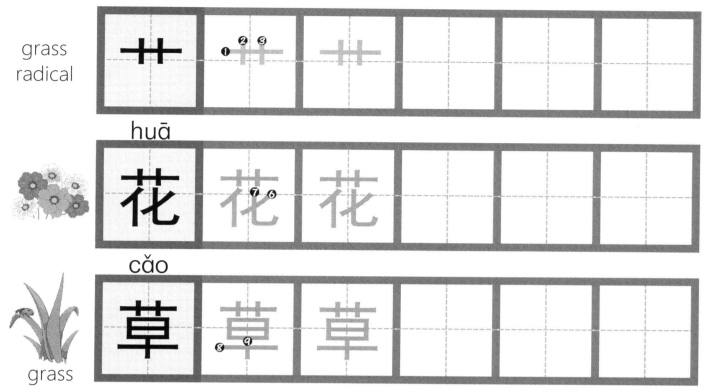

grass radical

huā

cǎo

grass

Find and trace ⺾ in these characters.

yuán

花园
garden

草地
lawn

lán

蓝天
blue sky

bái cài

白菜
Chinese cabbage

lù chá

绿茶

luó bo

萝卜
radish

Complete the characters with 艹 and color your favorite fruit!

cǎo　méi
早　每

lán　méi
监　每
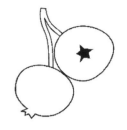

píng　guǒ
平　果

pú　táo
匍　匋

bō　luó
波　罗

xiāng　jiāo
香　焦

máng　guǒ
亡　果

mango

lì　zhī
劦　枝

lychee

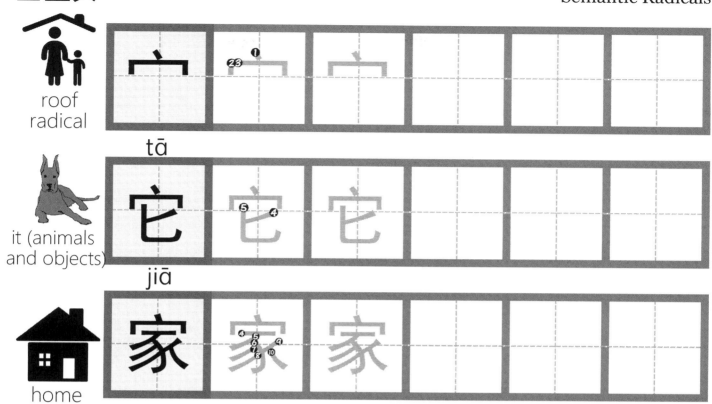

bǎogài
宝盖头

roof
radical

tā
它

it (animals
and objects)

jiā
家

home

Find and trace 宀 in these characters.

bǎo bao
小宝宝
baby

kè
客人
guest

ān
晚安

chǒng wù
宠物
pet

xiě zì
写字
write characters

huí
回家
go (back) home

57

What are they doing? Fill the blanks with the correct 他(们), 她(们), or 它(们). Remember 它 is for animals and objects.

哥哥在做什么？

____在踢球。
<small>tī</small>

姐姐在做什么？

____在写字。

爸爸妈妈在做什么？

_____在骑自行车。
<small>qí zì xíng chē</small>
<small>ride</small>

小猫在做什么？

____在捉蝴蝶。
<small>zhuō hú dié</small>
<small>catch butterfly</small>

shí
食字旁　　食 ➡ 饣

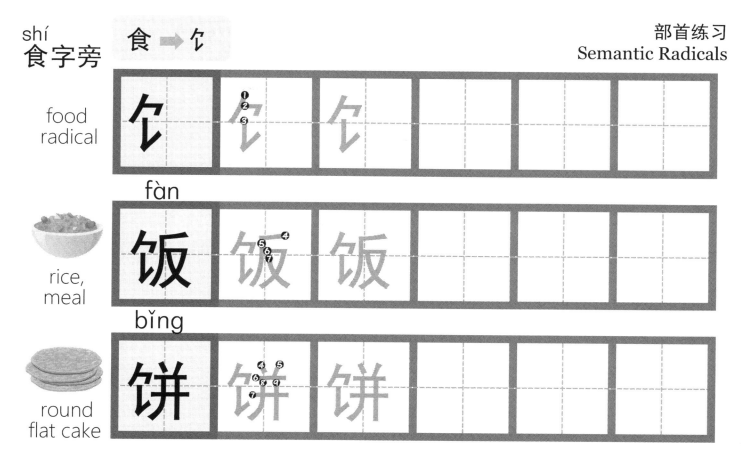

food radical

饣

fàn

饭

rice, meal

bǐng

饼

round flat cake

Find and trace 饣 in these characters.

米饭
rice

jiǎo
饺子
dumpling

è
饿了
hungry

bǎo
饱了
full

59

My Healthy Plate. Cut out the food and paste on the plate.

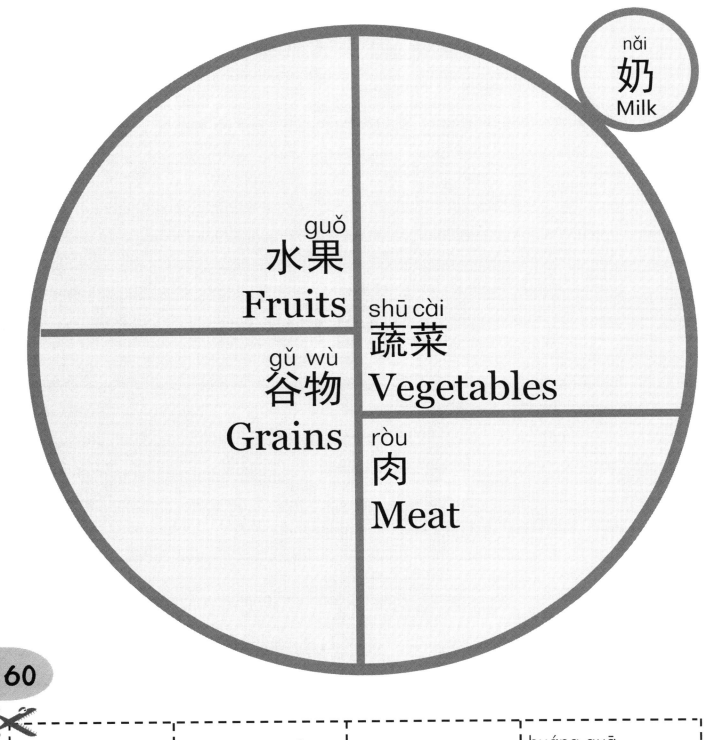

nǎi
奶
Milk

guǒ
水果
Fruits

shū cài
蔬菜
Vegetables

gǔ wù
谷物
Grains

ròu
肉
Meat

60

米饭

苹果

鸡肉

huáng guā
黄瓜

白菜

miàn tiáo
面条
noodles

xī
西瓜

luó bo
萝卜

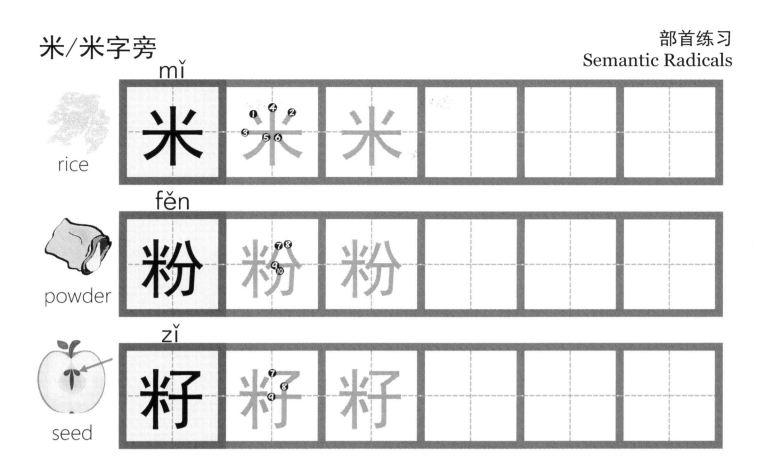

mǐ — rice
fěn — powder
zǐ — seed

Find and trace 米 in these characters.

zhōu
粥
porridge

táng
糖
candy, sugar

dàn gāo
蛋糕
cake

miàn fěn
面粉
FLOUR

奶粉
milk powder

bǐ
粉笔
chalk

Hidden Picture. Color the <u>boxes</u> by the code.

Characters with 米 = 棕色 (zōng) brown
Characters with ⺾ = 橙色 (chéng) orange
Characters with 彳 = 黄色
Characters with 宀 = 蓝色

		早						
		花		草		茶		
跑	找	家	打	字	扫	安	握	跳
		粉						
		饭						
		糖						
		饼						
		糕						
		雪						

它是什么？ What is it? Circle the correct word.

米饭　面包　蛋糕　饺子

衣/衣字旁/衣字底　衣 ➡ 衤

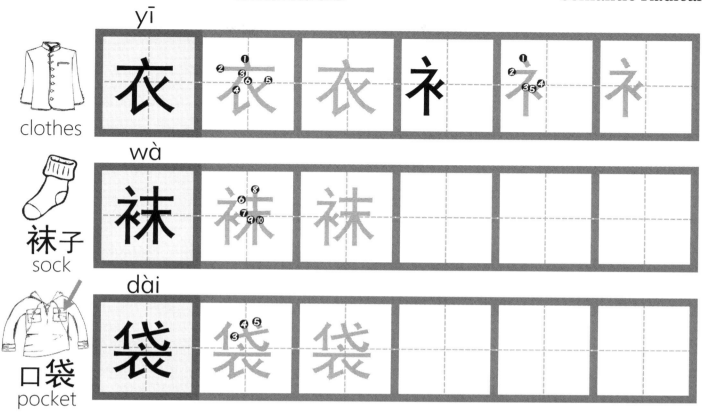

yī
衣
clothes

wà
袜
袜子
sock

dài
袋
口袋
pocket

Find and trace 衤/衣 in these characters.

chèn
衬衫

qún
裙子

kù
裤子

xiù
袖子
sleeve

máo
毛衣
sweater

mián ǎo
棉袄
cotton-padded jacket

Read and circle the characters that have 衤.

妹妹 穿 短 裙，姐姐穿长裙。
chuān duǎn
wear short

哥哥穿长裤。弟弟穿短裤。

爸爸穿长袖衬衫，妈妈穿短袖衬衫。

Riddle. 这 是什么 动 物？What animal is this?
zhè dòngwù

一只大老鼠，
lǎo shǔ

耳朵像小兔。
ěr duo xiàng tù
look like

肚上有口袋，
dù
belly

个高跳得快。
gè gāo tiào de kuài
(It is) tall (and) runs fast.

袋鼠

Turn the book upside down to see the answer.

虫/虫字旁/虫字底

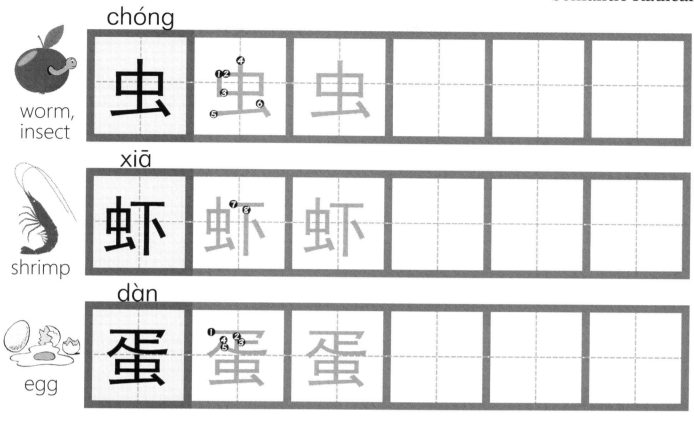

chóng
虫
worm, insect

xiā
虾
shrimp

dàn
蛋
egg

Find and trace 虫 in these characters.

qīng wā
青蛙

lóng
龙虾
lobster

páng xiè
螃蟹
crab

wō
蜗牛
snail

mì fēng
蜜蜂
bee

fēng mì
蜂蜜
honey

Many insects and reptiles have the 虫 radical in their names. Find and color 虫 in these words.

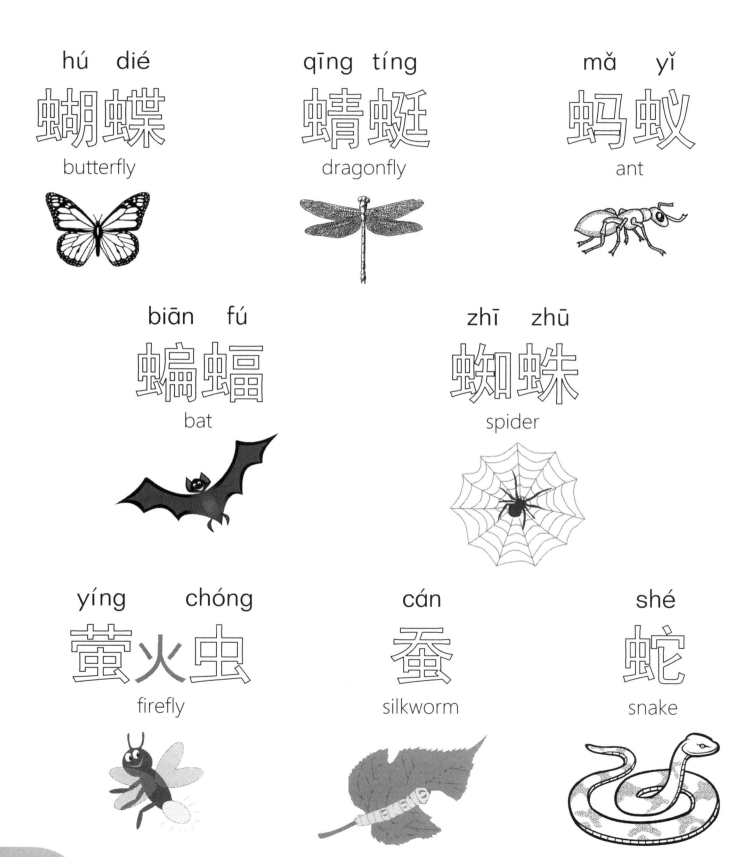

hú dié
蝴蝶
butterfly

qīng tíng
蜻蜓
dragonfly

mǎ yǐ
蚂蚁
ant

biān fú
蝙蝠
bat

zhī zhū
蜘蛛
spider

yíng chóng
萤火虫
firefly

cán
蚕
silkworm

shé
蛇
snake

鸟/鸟字旁/鸟字底

部首练习
Semantic Radicals

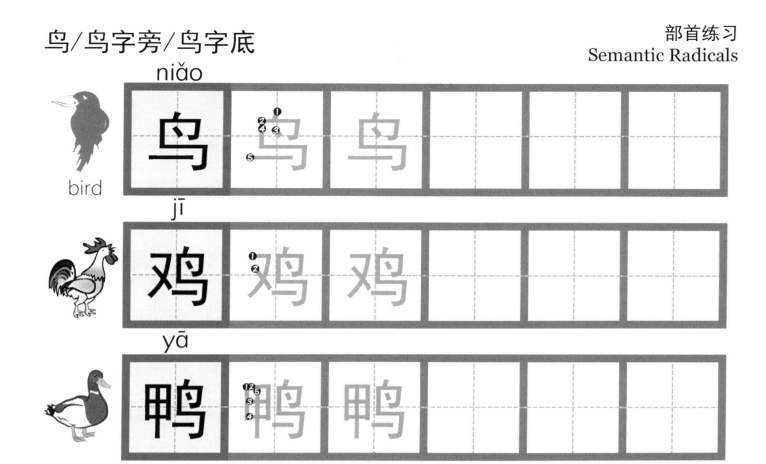

niǎo
鸟

bird

jī
鸡

yā
鸭

Find and trace 鸟 in these characters.

yīng wǔ
鹦鹉

parrot

é
天鹅

swan

qǐ
企鹅

penguin

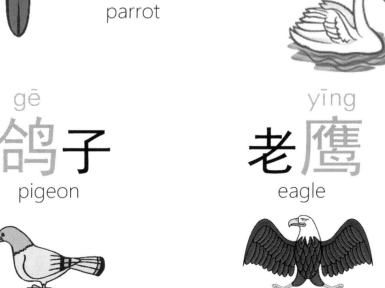

gē
鸽子

pigeon

yīng
老鹰

eagle

猫头鹰

owl

67

Read and draw.

1. 天黑了，鸡妈妈和小鸡回家了。
hēi — black, dark
huí

2. 一只蓝鸟在树上吃虫子。
lán

3. 两只黄鸭在小河里洗澡。
huáng
xǐ zǎo

68

fǎn quǎn
反 犬 旁　犬 ➡ 犭

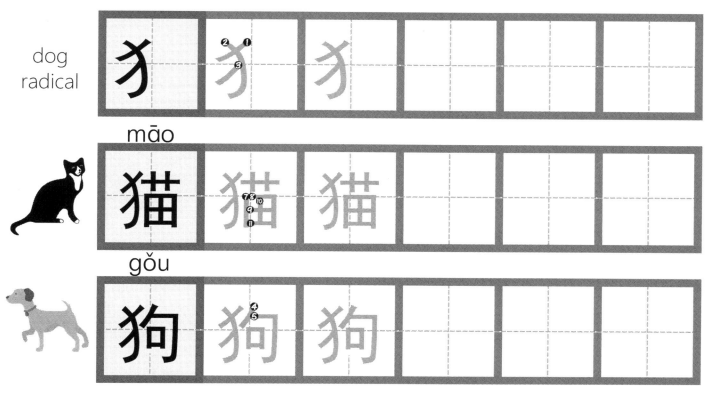

dog radical 犭

māo 猫

gǒu 狗

Find and trace 犭 in these characters.

hóu
猴子
monkey

láng
狼
wolf

xióng
熊猫
panda

zhū
猪
pig

shī
狮子
lion

hú li
狐狸
fox

liè
猎人
hunter

犭，虫，or 鸟？

Say the name of each animal in Chinese and match them with their radical.

虫	犭	鸟

Now you've learned 22 semantic radicals. Great job!

Radical	Variant	Examples	Radical	Variant	Examples
人	亻	会你他	土		地块坐
女		妈姐要	日		明春星
父		爸爷	雨	⻗	雪雷零
口		吃名只	艹		花草茶
手	扌	拿打找	宀		它家宝
足	𧾷	跑跳跟	食	饣	饭饼饿
目		眼睛看	米		粉籽糖
水	氵	江河海	衣	衤	袋袜裙
冫		冰冷凉	虫		虾蛇蛋
火		灯灰烫	鸟		鸡鸭鹰
木		杯板朵	犬	犭	猫狗狼

Quiz Time!

Match each radical with the correct picture. Draw a line.

亻	日
虫	口
扌	足
目	氵
宀	米
饣	艹

Write the character for each picture. Look at their radicals for hint.

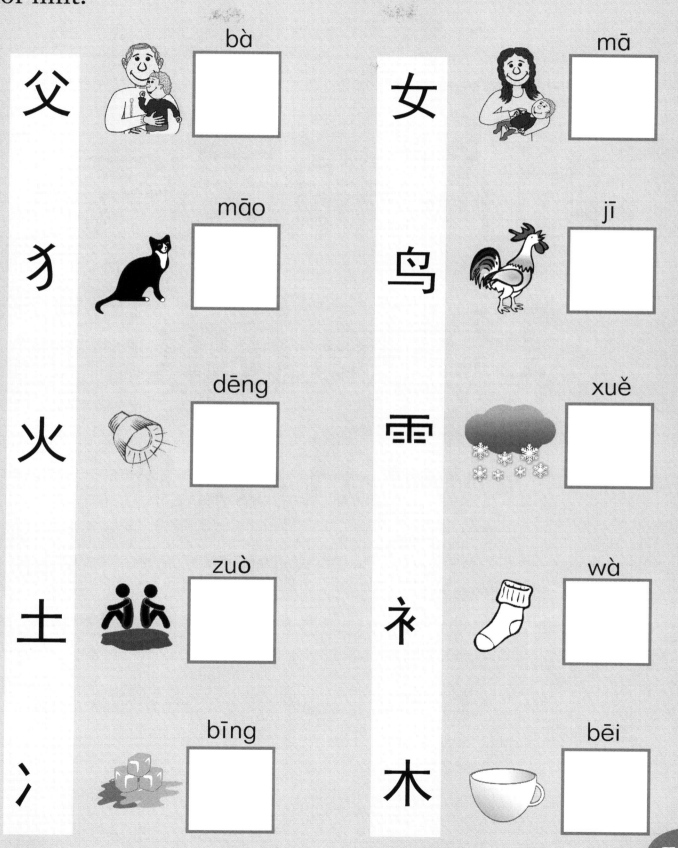

父

犭

火

土

冫

女

鸟

雨

衤

木

bà

mā

māo

jī

dēng

xuě

zuò

wà

bīng

bēi

时间和天气
Time and Weather

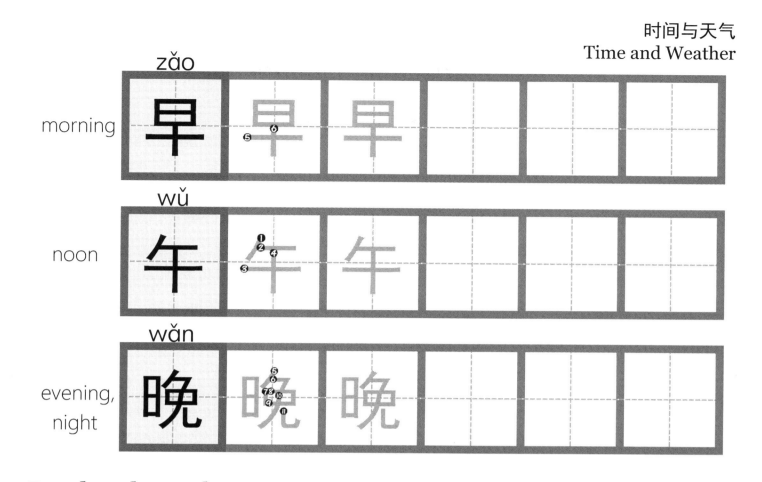

zǎo
morning
早

wǔ
noon
午

wǎn
evening, night
晚

Read and match.

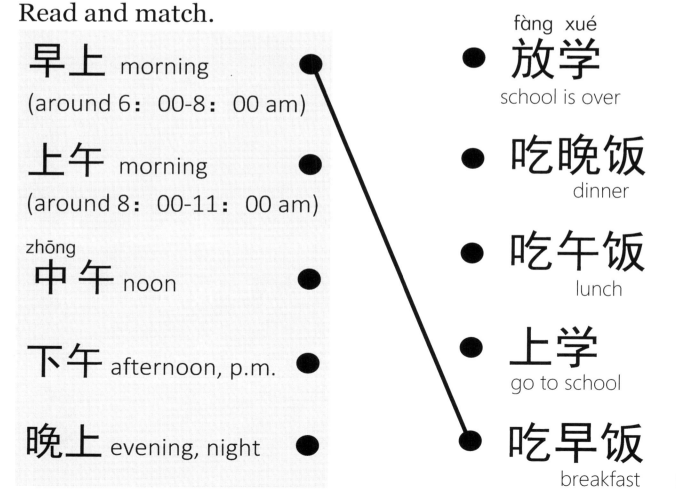

早上 morning
(around 6：00-8：00 am)

上午 morning
(around 8：00-11：00 am)

zhōng
中午 noon

下午 afternoon, p.m.

晚上 evening, night

fàng xué
放学
school is over

吃晚饭
dinner

吃午饭
lunch

上学
go to school

吃早饭
breakfast

Circle one or more time words for each activity.

早上
中午
晚上

shuā yá
刷牙

上午
中午
下午

吃午饭

早上
中午
晚上

zǎo
洗澡

上午
中午
晚上

shuì jiào
睡觉

早上
中午
晚上

chuān yī fu
穿衣服
put on   clothes

早上
下午
晚上

zuò zuò yè
做作业

xiàn zài
现 在 几点？　　What time is it now?

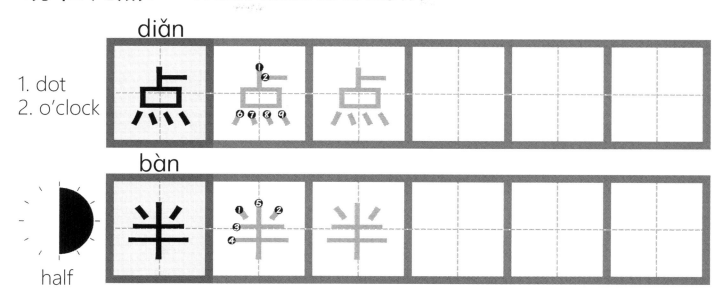

diǎn

1. dot
2. o'clock

点　点　点

bàn

半　半　半

half

Look at the clock and write down the time.

四点

十点半

Fill in the blanks with time. Use 点/半.

 早上＿＿＿＿＿＿我刷牙。

上午＿＿＿＿＿＿我上学。

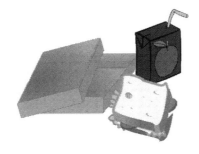 中午＿＿＿＿＿＿我吃饭。

下午＿＿＿＿＿＿我放学。

fàng

 晚上＿＿＿＿＿＿我睡觉。

fēn

1. minute
2. cent

分 分 分

Count by 5s and write down the number.

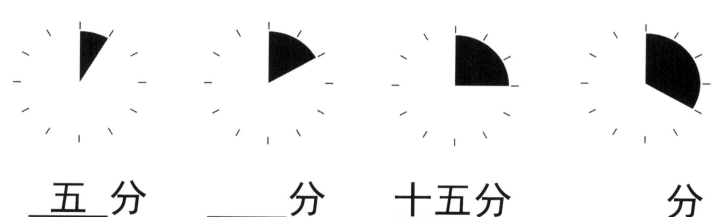

___五___ 分   _____分   十五分   _____分

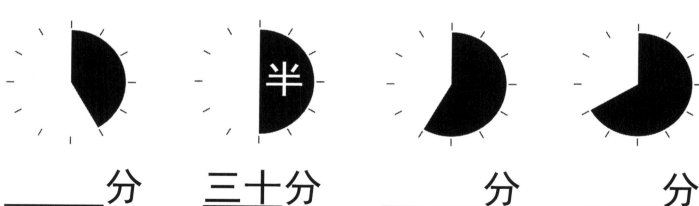

_____分   三十分   _____分   _____分

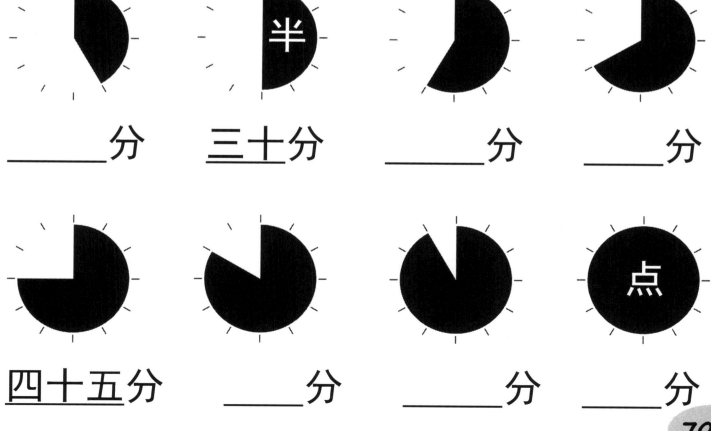

四十五分   _____分   _____分   _____分

Write the time in Chinese for each clock.

06: 00

12: 00

03: 00

六点

_____

_____

06: 08

12: 05

03: 01

líng
六点零八

___ 零 ___

___ 零 ___

08: 14

09: 19

11: 30

八点十四

_____

十一点半

04: 30

02: 47

10: 56

_____

两点四十七

_____

Read and match.

你好！我叫朋朋。我上一年级。我

^{nián jí}

go to 1st grade

^{měi}

每天早上七点刷牙，七点十分吃早饭。

everyday

^{xiào chē} ^{fàng}

七点半我坐校车上学。下午三点我放学，

school bus

晚上八点半睡觉。

| 07 : 00 |
| AM |

| 07 : 10 |
| AM |

| 07 : 30 |
| AM |

| 08 : 30 |
| PM |

四季 jì Four Seasons

chūn

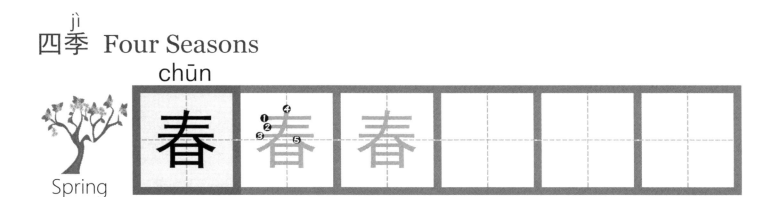

Spring

Read and draw.

三月，春暖花开。
nuǎn kāi
warm

我们去看花。
qù
go

三月
March

春暖花开：Flowers bloom in the warm spring.

Read and circle one or more activities you do in Spring.

春天你做什么？ 春天我＿＿＿。
<small>zuò</small>

种花
<small>zhòng</small>
plant

堆雪人
<small>duī</small>

扫树叶

骑自行车
<small>qí</small>

Circle what you would 穿 (wear clothes, shoes, and socks) and underline what you would 戴 (wear most accessories) for the activity.

骑自行车
<small>qí</small>

我 穿 〇 ，我戴＿＿＿。
<small>chuān</small>　<small>dài</small>

凉鞋
<small>liáng xié</small>
sandals

球鞋
tennis shoes

拖鞋
<small>tuō</small>
flip flops

皮鞋
<small>pí</small>
leather shoes

手套
<small>tào</small>

帽子
<small>mào</small>
hat

头盔
<small>kuī</small>
helmet

游泳眼镜
<small>jìng</small>
swimming goggles

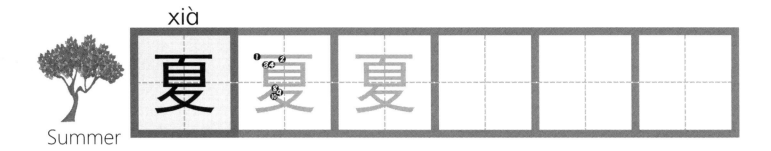

xià

夏　夏　夏

Summer

Read and draw.

　　　　　　　　yán
七月，夏日炎炎。

我们去游泳。

夏日炎炎：Summer days are burning hot.

Read and circle one or more activities you do in Summer.

夏天你做什么？　夏天我＿＿＿。

wán
玩水
play

fàng　zhēng
放风筝
fly a kite

游泳

堆雪人

Circle what you would 穿 and underline what you would 戴 for the activity.

游泳　　我穿（　　），我戴＿＿＿。

máo
毛衣

游泳衣

qún
裙子

chènshān
衬衫

tài yáng jìng
太阳镜
sunglasses

游泳眼镜

太阳帽

游泳帽

85

Fall

qiū
秋 秋 秋

Read and draw.

十月，秋高气爽。
qì shuǎng
air refreshing

我们去爬山。
pá
climb

秋高气爽：The weather in Fall is clear and refreshing.

Read and circle one or more activities you do in Fall.

秋天你做什么？　秋天我____。

zhòng
种花

堆雪人

跑步

扫树叶

Circle what you would 穿 and underline what you would 戴 for the activity.

跑步　　我穿 ，我戴____ 。

tuō xié
拖鞋

liáng
凉鞋

球鞋

皮鞋

tào
手套

biǎo
手表

jìng
游泳眼镜

kuī
头盔

87

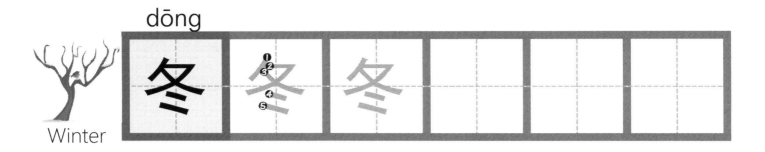

dōng

Winter

Read and draw.

十二月，冬雪飘飘。

piāo

float in the air

我们去堆雪人。

冬雪飘飘：Winter snow dances in the breeze.

Read and circle one or more activities you do in Winter.

冬天你做什么？　冬天我＿＿＿。

qí
骑自行车

wán
玩水

堆雪人

zhēng
放风筝

Circle what you would 穿 and underline what you would 戴 for the activity.

堆雪人　　我穿〇，我戴＿＿＿。

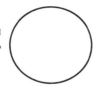

duǎn kù
短裤

mián ǎo
棉袄

qún
裙子

游泳衣

手表

手套

游泳帽

头盔

89

今天的天气怎么样？ How is the weather today?

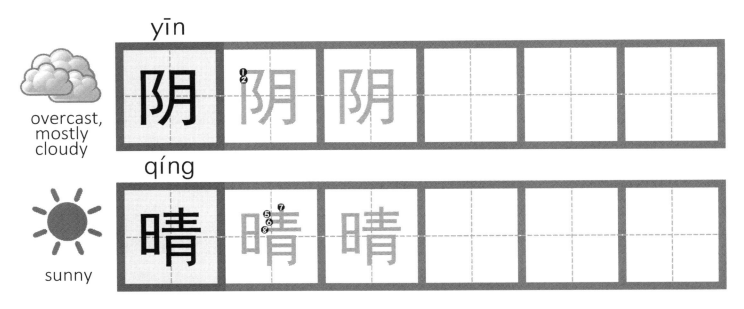

yīn
阴 阴 阴

qíng
晴 晴 晴

Look at the pictures and fill in the blanks with words from the word box.

天晴　　天阴　　下雨　　下雪

今天＿＿＿＿＿。

今天＿＿＿＿＿。

今天＿＿＿＿＿。

今天＿＿＿＿＿。

Look at the weather forecast and answer the questions.

一月五号	一月六号	一月七号	一月八号	一月九号	一月十号
多云 partly cloudy	天晴	天阴	小雨	大风	大雪

1. 一月五号的天气怎么样？

    天晴　　下雨　　多云　　有风

2. 一月六号下雨吗？　　下　　不下

3. 一月七号下雪吗？　　下　　不下

4. 一月八号雨大吗？　　大　　不大

5. 一月九号有风吗？　　有　　没有
                        méi

6. 一月十号冷吗？　　冷　　不冷

91

Quiz Time!

Look at each picture and write down the season.

Look at each picture and write down the weather.

反义词
Opposites

Fill in the blanks with opposites from the word box.

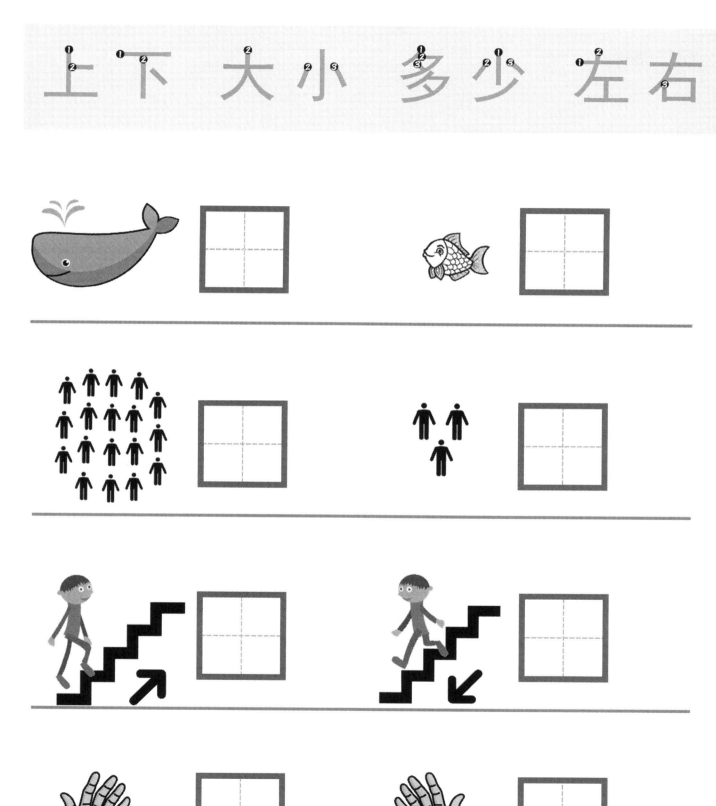

Draw a line between the opposites.

大人
adult

rè
热
hot

白天

fǎn
反
reverse,
opposite

kū
哭

hái
小孩
child

冷

yè
黑夜
night

zhèng
正
upright, correct

xiào
笑
smile

Fill in the blanks with opposites from the word box.

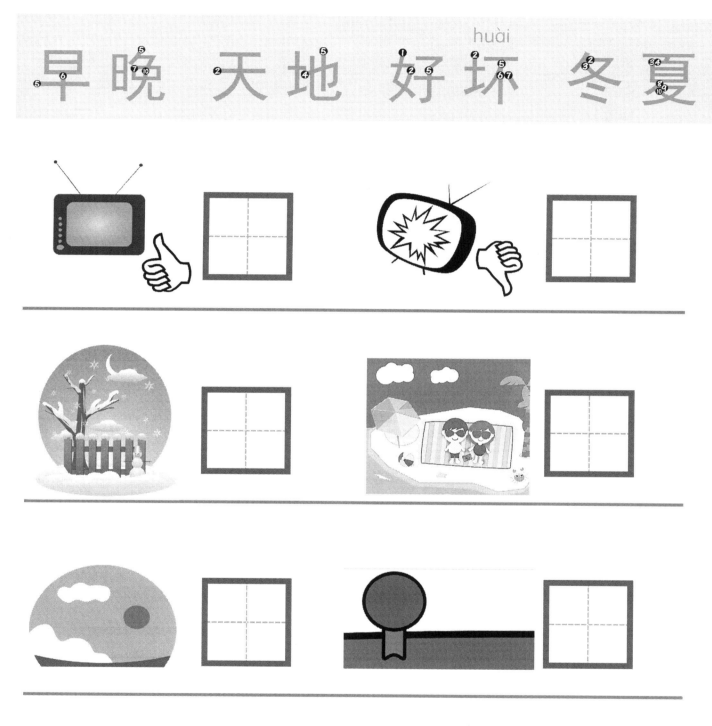

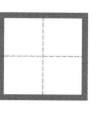

Draw a line between the opposites.

nán
男

kè
客人

chū
出
exit

女

晴

bǎo
饱

zhǔ
主人

雨

è
饿

rù
入
enter

98

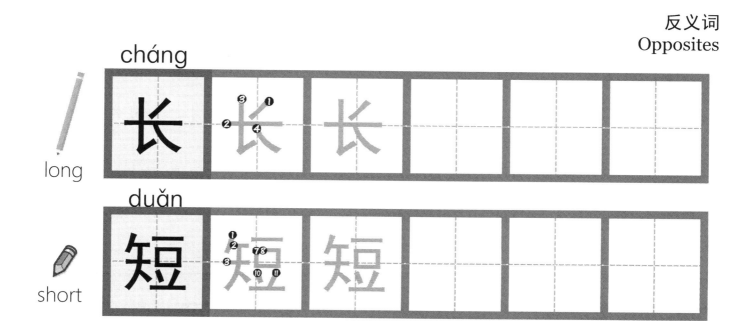

cháng
长 long

duǎn
短 short

Fill in the blanks with 长/短.

姐姐的头发_____。

tóu fa
hair

弟弟的头发____。

猴子的尾巴____。

wěi ba

兔子的尾巴____。

99

Fill in the blanks with 长/短.

 ____裙 qún

 ____裙

 ____裤 kù

 ____裤

 ____袜 wà

 ____袜

 ____袖 xiù 衬衫 chèn shān

 ____袖 衬衫

 ____毛狗 máo
hair, fur

 ____毛狗

100

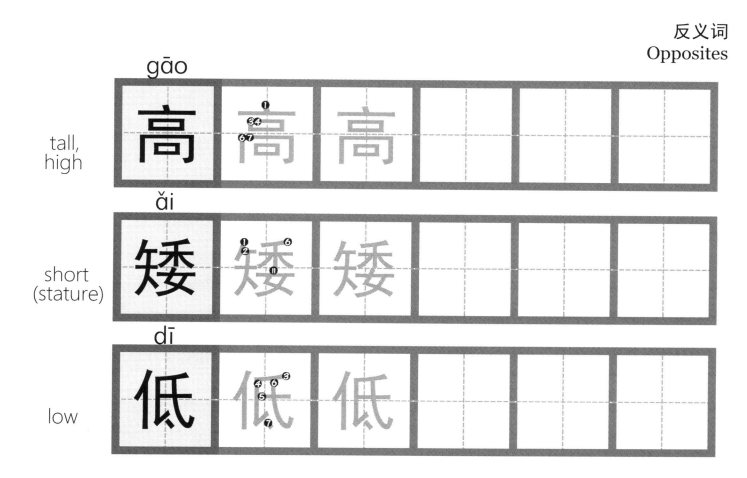

gāo
高

tall, high

ǎi
矮

short (stature)

dī
低

low

Fill in the blanks with 高/矮/低.

大人____，小孩____。

hái

jǐng lù
长颈鹿____，山羊____。

de
飞机飞得____。
The plane flies high.

mì fēng
蜜蜂飞得____。
low

101

Tall or short? Which is better? Read and retell this story.

长颈鹿和山羊 The Giraffe and the Goat
jǐng lù

长颈鹿高，山羊矮。

长颈鹿说："高好"，山羊说："矮好"。
shuō
say

他们来到一个花园。
lái dào
arrive at

长颈鹿可以吃到高高的树叶。
kě yǐ   eat   high   yè
can

山羊太矮，吃不到。
tài   can't reach
too

长颈鹿说："你看，高好吧？"
ba
Look, it's good to be tall, right?

山羊从花园的门走进去，
cóng   jìn
from   walk in

可以吃到矮矮的草。

长颈鹿太高，进不去。
can't get in

山羊说："你看，矮好吧？"

后来，长颈鹿拿来树叶，山羊拿来草。
hòu   ná
later   bring

他们一起吃，成了好朋友。
qǐ   chéng
together   become

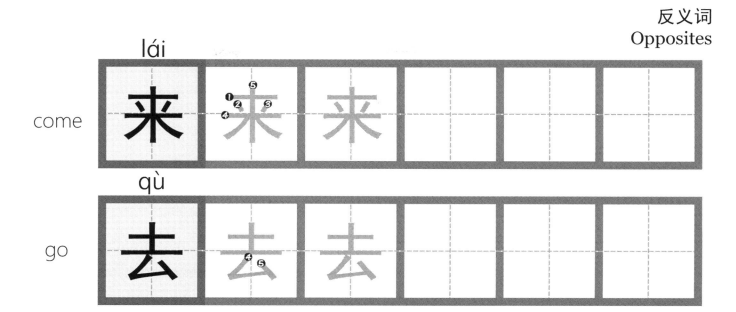

lái
come 来

qù
go 去

Fill in the blanks with 来/去.

妈妈：吃饭了！
明明：＿＿＿了！

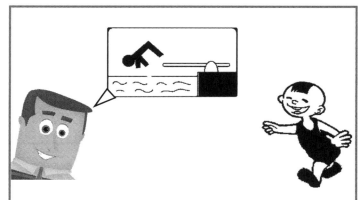

爸爸：去不去游泳？
明明：＿＿＿！

 小鱼在水里游<u>来</u>游<u>去</u>。
　　　　　　　　swim back and forth

 小鸟在天上飞＿＿＿飞＿＿＿。

 虫子在地上爬＿＿＿爬＿＿＿。

103

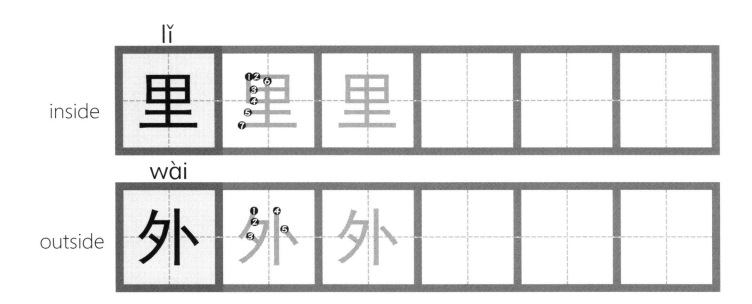

里 lǐ inside

外 wài outside

Read and draw.

1. 车里有两个人。

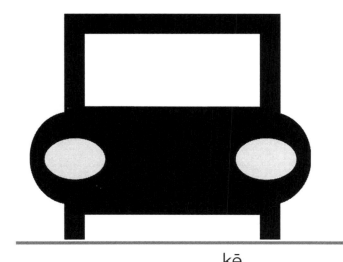

2. 门外有三棵树。
kē

3. 一只小猫在盒子里。
hé box

两只小鸡在盒子外。

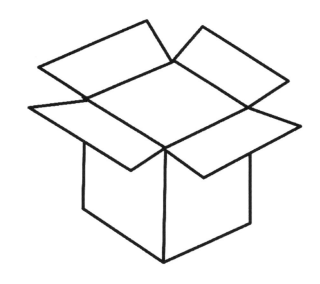

104

qián

front

前 前 前

hòu

back

后 后 后

Fill in the blanks with 前/后.

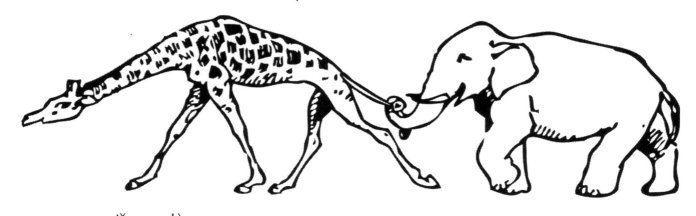

jǐng lù

长颈鹿在____，大象在____。

Color the pictures as directed.

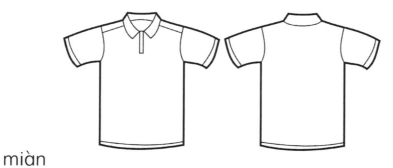

miàn

前面是红色，后面是蓝色。

front

105

Look at the calendar and fill in the date and day of the week for each day.

前天	zuó 昨天	今天	明天	后天
the day before yesterday	yesterday	today	tomorrow	the day after tomorrow
		二月三号		
星期	星期	qī 星期四 Thursday	星期	星期

Fill in the blanks with opposites from the word box.

高　矮　长　短　前　后

大象的鼻子 bí
鼻子____，猪的鼻子____。
nose

长颈鹿____，山羊____。
jǐng lù

肚子在___，尾巴在___。
dù
belly

Make your own dice of opposites!

反义词
Opposites

1. Cut off this page.
2. Cut along ———
3. Fold along - - - - -
4. Glue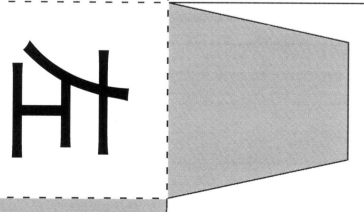
5. Play. Roll the dice and point to the direction as the word says.

This page has been left blank.

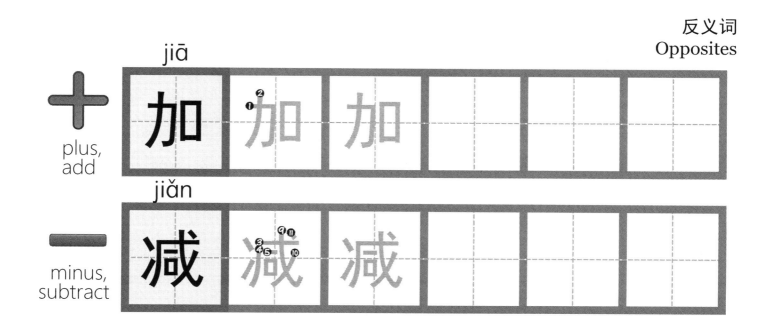

jiā

加 加 加

plus, add

jiǎn

减 减 减

minus, subtract

Read, translate, and answer.

1. 一加一等于几？   `1 + 1 = 2`

(děng yú jǐ — equal)

2. 四加七等于几？

3. 十五加九等于几？

4. 八减三等于几？

5. 十减六等于几？

6. 十九减二等于几？

Radical additions and subtractions. 什么字？

1. 日 加 月 是什么字？

$$日 + 月 = 明$$

2. 木 加 不 是什么字？

3. 虫 加 下 是什么字？

4. 日 加 十 是什么字？

5. 亻 加 木 是什么字？

6. 冰 减去 冫 是什么字？
　　　(take away)

$$冰 - 冫 =$$

7. 们 减去 亻 是什么字？

8. 妈 减去 女 是什么字？

9. 草 减去 艹 是什么字？

10. 字 减去 宀 是什么字？

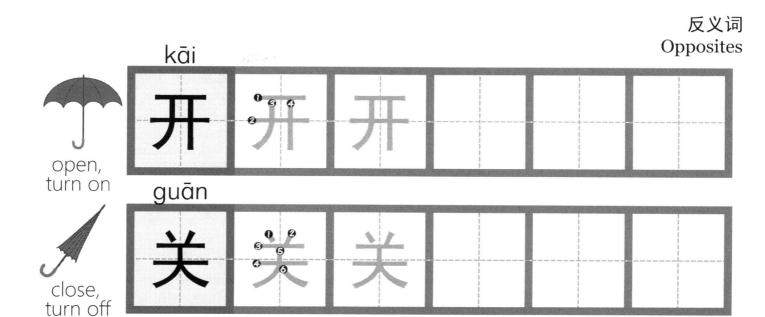

kāi
开 — open, turn on

guān
关 — close, turn off

Fill in the blanks with 开/关 or 打开/关上.

开 ←→ 关

开门 ←→ ＿门

＿灯 ←→ 关灯

打开 ←→ 关上

bǎ
把门打开 ←→ 把门＿＿＿＿

把灯＿＿＿＿ ←→ 把灯关上

diàn shì
把电视打开 ←→ 把电视＿＿＿＿

Quiz Time!

Look, draw, and write the opposites.

⬆️ 上	⬇️
⬅️ 左	
	➖ 减
☂️ 开	
	✏️ 短

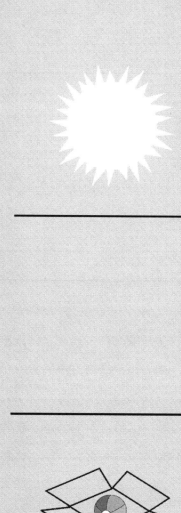 晴

 矮

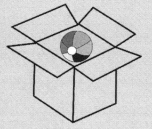 里

 坏

 男

疑问词
Question Words

shuí
谁
who

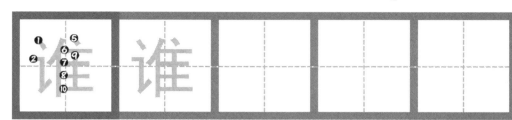

Look, ask, and answer.

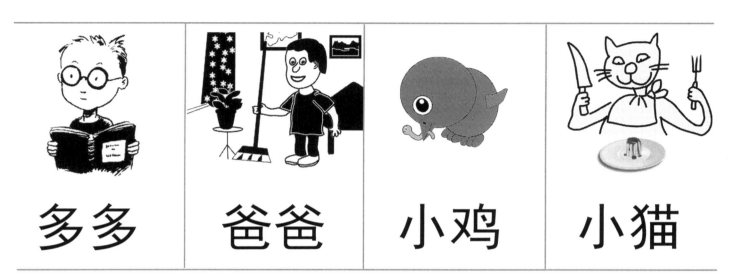

| 多多 | 爸爸 | 小鸡 | 小猫 |

1. <u>谁</u> 在看书？ _____在看书。

2. ___在扫地？ _____在扫地。

ài
3. ___爱吃虫子？ _____爱吃虫子。
love

4. ___吃了弟弟的蛋糕？

_____吃了他的蛋糕。

115

谁的？ Whose?

Look, read, and match.

谁的鼻子长？
bí

谁的牙齿尖？
chǐ jiān
teeth sharp

谁的尾巴短？
wěi

这是谁的袜子？

谁的名字叫多多？

这是谁的脚印？
jiǎo yìn
footprint

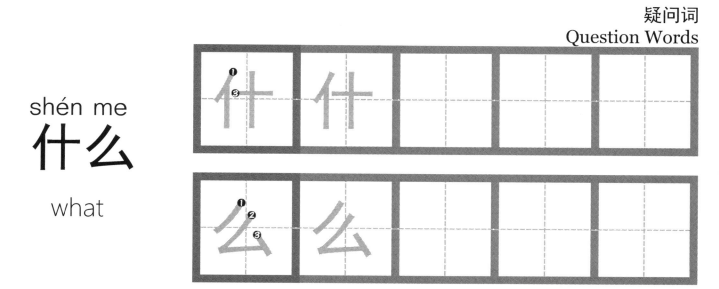

shén me
什么
what

Fill in the blanks with 什么 and circle the correct answers.

1. 天上有_____?

月亮　　太阳　　星星

2. 地里有_____?

　cài　　　xiāng jiāo　　　luó　bo
白菜　　香蕉　　萝卜

　　　　　dòng wù　　　　　　shuì jiào
3. _____动物晚上不睡觉?

　　　　　　　　　　yīng
鸡　　　狗　　　猫头鹰

　　　　　zhuō lǎo shǔ
4. _____动物捉老鼠?

山羊　　猫　　大象

117

Answer the questions in Chinese, English, or pictures.

1. 你叫什么名字？我叫＿＿＿＿＿。

2. 你喜欢什么颜色？我喜欢＿＿＿色。

xǐ huan（like）　　yán sè（color）

3. 你爱吃什么水果？我爱吃＿＿＿＿＿＿。

Read and match.

什么动物叫"喵喵"？

dòng wù　miāo

小羊

什么动物叫"咩咩"？

miē

企鹅

qǐ é

什么鸟不会飞？

萤火虫

yíng

什么虫会发光？

fā（glow）

小猫

jǐ
几

how many
(usually for less
than 10)

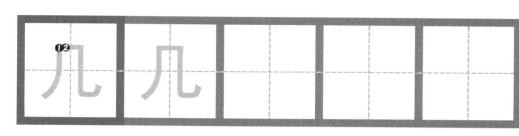

Count the numbers of cows, sheep, and horses that Old
McDonald has on his farm.

nóngchǎng
农　场 里有<u>几头牛</u>？<u>几只羊</u>？<u>几匹马</u>？
farm

有＿＿头牛，＿＿只羊，＿＿匹马。

119

Answer the questions in Chinese.

1. 三加六等于^{děng yú}几？　　等于＿＿＿。

1. 三加六等于几？　　等于＿＿＿。

2. 十减四等于几？　　等于＿＿＿。

3. 你几岁^{suì}？　　　　我＿＿＿＿＿＿。

4. 你每^{měi}天几点上学？我每天＿＿点上学。

5. 你上几年级^{jí}？　　　我上＿＿＿年级。

6. 一年有几个季节^{jì jié}？一年有＿＿个季节。
   seasons

7. 一个星期有几天？一个星期有＿＿天。

8. 今天是几月几号？星期几？

   今天是＿＿＿＿＿＿＿＿＿，星期＿＿＿。

duō shǎo
多少

how many
(usually for more
than 10),
how much

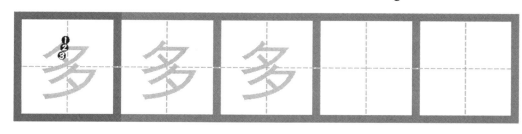

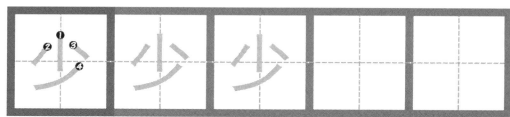

Complete the questions with 多少.

bān

1. 你们班有＿＿＿个学生？
class   xué sheng / students

我们班有十九个学生。

2. 一年有＿＿＿天？

一年有三百六十五天。

Complete the questions with 几岁 or 多大.
(for kids)   (for adults)

你妹妹今年＿＿＿？她今年三岁。

你爸爸今年＿＿＿？他今年三十八岁。

121

多少钱？ How much (money)?
qián

kuài

1. chunk,
2. dollar

块 块 块

máo

1. fur,
2. dime

毛 毛 毛

Write out the numbers in Chinese.

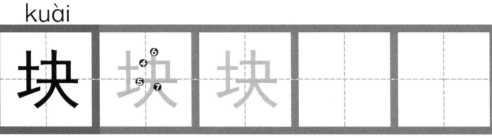

一块＝十毛   一毛＝十分

$1.00	$3.00	$2.10	$7.60
一块	_____	两块一	_____

10¢	40¢	25¢	99¢
一毛	_____	两毛五	_____

5¢	8¢	$1.99	$2.88
五分	_____	一块九毛九	_____

Look, read, and answer. Use 块/毛.

1.
zhè shuāng xié
这 双 鞋多少钱？
this pair of shoes
二十五____。

$25.00

2. 这个书包多少钱？

____ ____ ____。

$19.00

3.
xiāng jiāo
香 蕉多少钱一磅？
bàng
per pound
四____九一磅。

49¢/lb

4. 西瓜多少钱一个？

三___八___九一个。

$3.89/ea

nǎ lǐ
哪里
where

哪　哪　哪

足球在哪里？
soccer

zhè
足球在这里。
here

xiē
这些东西在哪里？
Where are these items? Find and color them in the picture.

床　　书包　　电视　　水杯　　裤子　　球鞋

Complete the questions with 哪里.

1. 星星在_____?
   星星在树上。
   女孩在_____?
   女孩在树下。

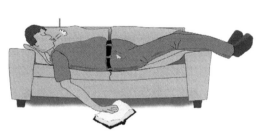

2. 爸爸在_____?
   爸爸在沙发^{shā fā}上。
   书在_____?
   书在爸爸手里。

3. 老鼠在_____?
   老鼠在冰箱^{xiāng}里。
   猫在_____?
   猫在冰箱上。

125

哪 (一) 个？ Which one? 哪些？ Which ones?

Read and match.

1. 哪一个是老师？

2. 哪些是学生？

3. 哪个是医生？

4. 哪个是警察？

哪 (一) 天？ Which day?

1. 哪一天是圣诞节？ ____月_____号。
   Christmas

2. 哪天是新年？ _____。
   new year

3. 哪天是你的生日？ _____。
   birthday

zěn

怎么

how

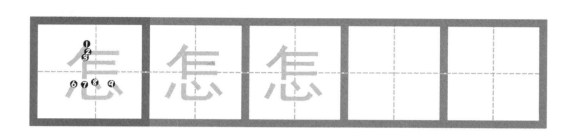

Read the question and circle your answer.

你每天怎么去上学？

 坐校车   坐火车

tiě
坐地铁   qì
subway   坐汽车

gōng jiāo
 坐公交车   chuán
bus   坐船
ship, boat

 走路   qí
骑自行车

怎么了？ **What happened? Read and circle.**

1. 哥哥怎么了？

他睡觉了。　他摔倒了。
shuāi dǎo
fall down

2. 弟弟怎么了？

diào
他的牙掉了。　他饿了。
fall out

Complete the questions with 怎么了.

1. 小猫_____?

dào
它们找不到妈妈了。
can't find

shì
2. 电视_____?

电视坏了。

怎么办？ What to do? Read and circle.
bàn

1. 下雨了怎么办？

戴眼镜　　打球　　打伞
dài　jìng

2. 下雪了怎么办？

戴手表　穿棉袄　穿短裤
biǎo　mián ǎo　kù

3. 生病了怎么办？
shēngbìng
get　sick

找警察　去公园　看医生
jǐng chá　　　　　yī
　　　　　　　　　　see

4. 天黑了怎么办？

开灯　开门　开电视

129

wèi

为什么

why

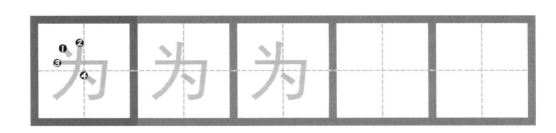

Complete the questions with 为什么.

1. 妹妹＿＿＿＿＿＿哭？
她肚子饿了。

2. 弟弟＿＿＿＿＿哭？
shuāi dǎo
他摔倒了。

3. 小猫＿＿＿＿＿叫？
它们找不到妈妈了。

4. 云云＿＿＿＿＿没上学？
bìng
她今天生病了。

yīn
因为
because

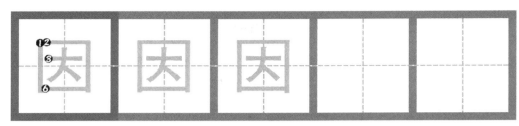

Answer the questions with 因为.

1. 今天为什么不上学？

_____今天是星期天。

2. 为什么夏天穿短裤？

_____夏天热。

3. 树叶为什么黄了？

_____秋天来了。

4. 天为什么黑了？

_____太阳下山了。

131

Quiz Time!

You've got a letter! Read and circle the correct answer.

你好！我叫冰冰。我今年六岁，我上一年级。我的家在 zhōng guó 中国。我每天坐 gōng jiāo 公交车上学，我的 bān 班里有三十五个小朋友。

1. 他叫什么名字？　　　　水水　　　　冰冰

2. 他几岁？　　　　　　　六岁　　　　七岁

3. 他上几年级？　　　　　二年级　　　一年级

4. 他的家在哪里？　　　　中国　　　　měi 美国
United States

5. 他每天怎么上学？　　　坐校车　　　坐公交车

6. 他的班里有多少个小朋友？　25 个　　　35 个

132

Now draw and write about yourself. Use English for words that you don't know in Chinese.

你好！我叫＿＿＿＿＿。我今年

＿＿＿岁。我上＿＿年级。我的家在

＿＿＿＿＿，我每天＿＿＿＿＿上学，

我的班里有＿＿＿＿＿个小朋友。

最常用字
Sight Words

yě

too,
also

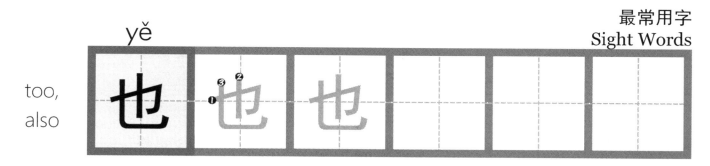

Copycat！弟弟 always wants the same thing that 哥哥 wants. Fill the blanks with 也.

 哥哥

 弟弟

è
我饿了。

我＿＿＿饿了！

yào
我要吃饺子。
want

我＿＿＿要吃饺子！

我要五个。

我＿＿＿要五个！

我饱了。

我＿＿＿饱了！

gōngyuán
我要去公园。
park

我＿＿＿要去公园！

我六岁。

我也六岁！

ò   duì
哦，不对，我四岁。
Oh   not right

135

Read and draw.

1. 你喜欢什么颜色？
   xǐ huan — like   yán sè — color

   我喜欢 [　　] ，也喜欢 [　　] 。

2. [　　] 是水果，[　　] 也是水果。

3. [　　] 会飞，[　　] 也会飞。

4. 我早上 [　　] ，晚上也 [　　] 。

Riddle. 这是什么？ What is this?

你哭他也哭，你笑他也笑，
你问他是谁，他说你知道。
wèn — ask   shuō — say   zhī dào — know

镜子
jìng

Turn the book upside down to see the answer.

dōu

都 都 都

all, both

Fill in the blanks with 都.

1. 他的爸爸和妈妈＿＿＿是中国人。

2. 我和妹妹＿＿＿喜欢画画。
　　　　　　　　huà

3. 蝙蝠和猫头鹰＿＿＿喜欢晚上。
　 biān fú 　　　　 yīng
　 bat 　　　　　 owl

4. 青蛙、鸭子和鱼＿＿＿会游泳。
　 qīng wā

5. 苹果和香蕉＿＿＿是水果。
　　　　　 jiāo

6. 六月、七月和八月＿＿＿是夏天。

7. 今天和明天＿＿＿不下雨。

137

也 or 都？

Fill in the blanks.

1. 我爱吃草莓，哥哥＿＿爱吃草莓。 ^{méi}

   我们＿＿爱吃草莓。

2. 蜜蜂会飞，蝴蝶＿＿会飞。 ^{mì fēng} ^{hú dié}

   蜜蜂和蝴蝶＿＿会飞。

3. 今天不下雪，明天＿＿不下雪。

   ＿＿ ＿＿ 和 ＿＿ ＿＿ ＿＿不下雪。

4. 牛吃草，羊＿＿吃草。

   牛＿＿羊＿＿ 吃草。

yòng

use

用 用 用

Fill in the blanks with 用 and match the activities with the correct body parts.

我 _用_ 眼睛

我 ____ 耳朵
ěr duo

我 ____ 鼻子
bí

我 ____ 嘴巴
zuǐ

我 ____ 手

我 ____ 脚
jiǎo
foot

wén xiāng
闻花香。
smell fragrance
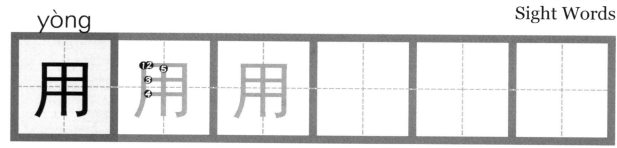

huà
画画。

yīn yuè
听音乐。
music

bù
跑步。

看书。

dōng xi
吃东西。
things

139

Draw a line from each word to the matching face part. Use the word box for hint.

头发

眉毛 (méi)

耳朵

眼睛

嘴巴

鼻子

牙齿 (chǐ)

舌头 (shé)

下巴

头发	眼睛	鼻子	眉毛	牙齿

舌头	下巴	嘴巴	耳朵
	 chin		

140

zuò

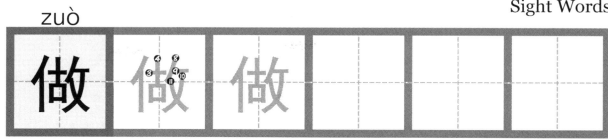

do,
make,
be

Complete the words with 做.

___饭

make a meal
(cook)

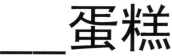

___蛋糕

make   a cake

___手工

make handcrafts

zuò yè

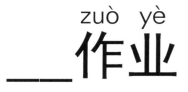

___作业

do   homework

___朋友

be   friends

kè

___客

be a guest

141

Read and circle your answer.

1. 放_{fàng}学了，你做什么？
after school

做作业　　踢球　　画画　　看书

2. 在家里，你帮_{bāng}爸爸妈妈做什么？
help

扫_{sǎo}地　　拖_{tuō}地　　擦_{cā}桌_{zhuō}子　　扔_{rēng}垃_{lā}圾_{jī}

3. 星期六和星期天你做什么？

上中文学校　　做作业　　游泳

踢球　　　去公园　　　在家睡觉

4. 你用眼睛做什么？

听声音　看书　看电视　闻_{wén}花香_{xiāng}

Read and circle your answer.

1. 放学了，你做什么？
(fàng = 放; after school = 放学)

做作业　　踢球　　画画　　看书

2. 在家里，你帮爸爸妈妈做什么？
(bāng = 帮; help)

扫地　　拖地　　擦桌子　　扔垃圾
(sǎo)　(tuō)　(cā zhuō)　(rēng lā jī)

3. 星期六和星期天你做什么？

上中文学校　　做作业　　游泳

踢球　　　去公园　　　在家睡觉

4. 你用眼睛做什么？

听声音　看书　看电视　闻花香
(wén)　(xiāng)

cóng

从

follow, from

dào

到

get to, reach, arrive

从…到… From…to…

Read and write/trace.

从一写到十.

从 A 写到 G.

从左写到右。

从上写到下。

从家到学校怎么走？
Help the boy find his way from home to school.

家

学校

Extend the words with 到 and complete the sentences with the words in the word box.

1. 看 → 看到   我＿＿＿＿＿天上有星星。
   look   see

2. 听 → 听到   我＿＿＿＿＿树上小鸟叫。
   listen hear

   wén
3. 闻 → 闻到   我闻＿＿＿蛋糕的 香 味。
   smell smell   xiāng wèi
                                    fragrance

4. 找 → 找到   我＿＿＿＿＿一个好朋友。
   look for find

Read and answer the questions at the end.

lí qù lǚ xíng
一只海狸去旅行 A Beaver Goes on a Trip

海狸，海狸，
你用耳朵做什么？

shēng yīn
我用耳朵听 声 音。
sound

你听到什么声音？

chàng gē
我听到大海在唱 歌。
sing a song

听声音

海狸，海狸，
你用鼻子做什么？

qì wèi
我用鼻子闻 气味。
scent

你闻到什么气味？

我闻到花的香味。

闻气味

海狸，海狸，
你用眼睛做什么？

dōng xi
我用眼睛看 东 西。
things

你看到什么东西？

我看到红色的云。

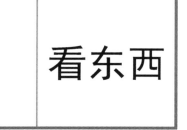

看东西

145

海狸，海狸，
你用嘴巴做什么？
　　我用嘴巴来 说 话。 shuō huà / talk
你说了什么？
　　我说，"你好，大海！"

说话

海狸，海狸，
你用 双 手做什么？ shuāng / pair (both)
　　我用双手拿东西。 ná / take, carry
你拿着什么东西？ zhe / carrying
　　我拿着我的行李。 xíng li / luggage

拿东西

海狸，海狸，
你用双脚做什么？ jiǎo
　　我用双脚来走路。 lù / walk
你要走路去哪儿？
　　我要走路去 旅行。 lǚ xíng / travel

走路

Which part of the body does the beaver use for each activity? Draw in the boxes.

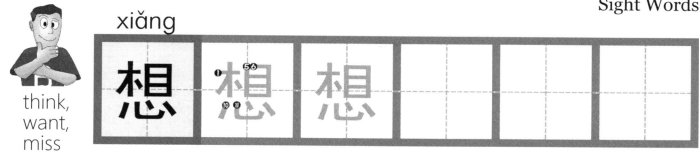

xiǎng

想　想　想

think,
want,
miss

What do they want to do? Fill in the blanks with 想 and
match the feelings with the desires.

kě
小猫渴了，
thirsty

它＿＿睡觉。

hóu kùn
小猴困了，
sleepy

gùn
他＿＿吃冰棍。
popsicle

弟弟饿了，

它＿＿喝水。

女孩冷了，

他＿＿吃饭。

男孩热了，

huí
她＿＿回家。

147

Read and answer the question below.

妹妹不睡觉

妹妹，你为什么不睡觉？

――我想妈妈。（妈妈来陪她。）

miss *accompany* (péi)

妹妹，你为什么还不睡觉？

(hái) *still*

――我想爸爸。（爸爸来陪她。）

妹妹，你为什么还不睡觉？

――我想哥哥。（哥哥来陪她。）

妹妹，你为什么还不睡觉？

(qí lín)

――我想吃冰淇淋。

want

妹妹！！！

Circle all that apply. 妹妹为什么不睡觉？

她想妈妈。　　　　她想爸爸。

她想哥哥。　　　　她想吃冰淇淋。

148

yào

want,
going to

要 要 要

Help the waiter find food for each customer. Fill in the
blanks with 要 and match the sentences with the pictures.

 你好！你要什么？

 我___四个饺子。

 我___一个冰淇淋。
      qí lín

 我___一杯绿茶。
      lǜ chá

 我___两块饼干。
       gān

 我___一杯果汁，不要加冰。
       zhī

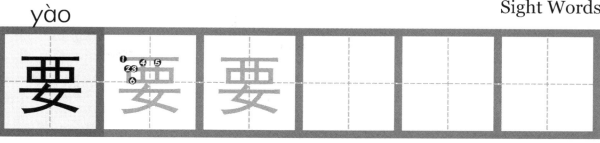

149

^{zhǎng}
长 *大了，你要做什么? What do you want to do when you grow up? Read and circle.

1. 长大了，我要当^{dāng}_____。
work as

^{yī}
医生

^{lǎo shī}
老师

^{chú}
厨师
chef

^{jǐng chá}
警察

球星

^{bǎn}
老板
boss

^{yīn yuè}
音乐家
musician

^{huà}
画家
artist

2. 长大了，我要_____。

开汽车^{qì}   开火车   开飞机   开飞船^{chuán}

去中国   去月球   去火星

150 *长: 1. cháng (meaning long), 2. zhǎng (meaning to grow).

bǐ

比 比 比

compare, than

Compare and circle the correct words.

1. 西瓜比苹果 大 小 。

2. 冬天比夏天 热 冷 。

3. 女孩比男孩 头发长 头发短 。

4. 长颈鹿比山羊 高 矮 。
（jǐng lù）

5. 多多六岁，云云七岁。

   多多比云云 大一岁 小一岁 。

151

Read, look, and draw.

yuán xíng
圆形 有三个。
circle (shape)

jiǎo
三角形比圆形多一个。

qīng tíng
蜻蜓飞得低。

小鸟比蜻蜓飞得高。

zhèng fāng
正方形有五个。

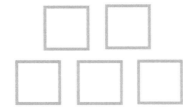

xīn
心形比正方形少两个。

tù   wěi ba
兔子尾巴短。

hóu
猴子比兔子尾巴长。

méi

没有

1. have not,
2. not as

没 没 没

Fill in the blanks with 没有.

1. Have not/ (There is) no

天上＿＿ ＿＿鱼。

今天＿＿ ＿＿雨，也＿＿ ＿＿雪。

2. Not as

苹果＿＿ ＿＿西瓜大。

弟弟＿＿ ＿＿姐姐头发长。

山羊＿＿ ＿＿长颈鹿个子高。

秋天＿＿ ＿＿冬天冷。

153

Quiz Time!

Fill in the blanks with words from the word box.

也　都　用　做　从...到...　要　比　没有

1. 小鸡和小鸭____吃虫子。

2. 他的眼睛是黑色，头发 ____是黑色。

3. 我会____一写____十。

4. 我____眼睛看书。

5. 长大了，我____去中国。

6. 哥哥____弟弟大三岁。弟弟____ ____哥哥高。

7. 我想和你____朋友。

Fun Time!

Can you find the pattern? Cut, paste, and read.

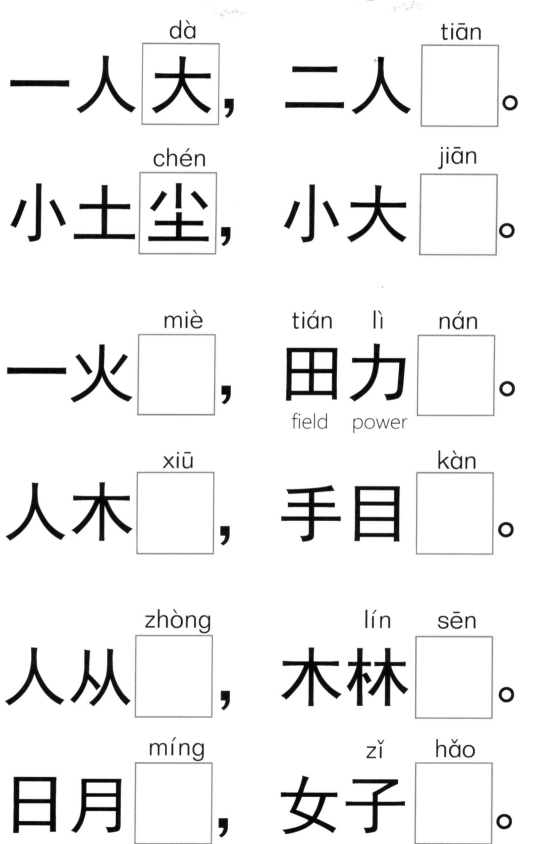

一人 大(dà)， 二人 ⬚(tiān)。

小土 尘(chén)， 小大 ⬚(jiān)。

一火 ⬚(miè)， 田(tián) 力(lì) ⬚(nán)。
field power

人木 ⬚(xiū)， 手目 ⬚(kàn)。

人从 ⬚(zhòng)， 木林 ⬚(sēn)。

日月 ⬚(míng)， 女子 ⬚(hǎo)。

天 男 尖 灭 明 看 众 森 好 休

155

答案
Answers

（For questions not included, answers may vary.）

Color each character with one color.

人 天 日
月 女 手

5

Color more Single-Component Characters.

木 水 火 土
山 雨 虫 米

6

Color each character with 2 colors.

7

好 妈 你
他 朋 和

8

尖 字 花
笑 四 圆

9

爬 过 看
尾 勺 可

10

网 匹

Color each character with 3 colors.

树 脚 鼻 茶

11

Circle 女 (female) in these characters.

妈 姐 她

Circle 犭 (animals that look like dogs) in these characters.

猫 狗 猪

13

Can you find the semantic radical in these characters? Color in their blocks.

zhōu   kan   pa
粥   看   爬

16

Find and trace 人 in these characters.

全班 合唱
观众 打伞
金鱼会游泳

17

What is he/ she doing? Find and trace 亻.

他在做什么?
他在休息。
她在做什么?
她在做作业。

20

Find and trace 女 in these words.

姐姐 妹妹
阿姨 姑姑
外婆 奶奶

21

Look at the pictures, and fill in the blanks.

爸爸的妈妈是 奶奶 ,
妈妈的 妈妈 是外婆。
爸爸的爸爸是 爷爷 ,
妈妈的 爸爸 是外公。

24

Find and trace 口 in these characters.

右 后 哥哥 哭

25

Find and trace 口 in these characters.

吃饭   喝水   舌头
吹泡泡 三月五号 嘴巴

Find and trace 扌 in these characters

扫地   拖地   找朋友
拍球   扔球   接球

31

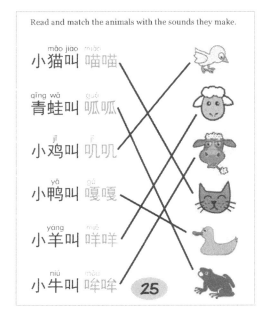

Read and match the animals with the sounds they make.

小猫叫 māo jiāo 喵喵 miāo
青蛙叫 qīng wā 呱呱 guā
小鸡叫 jī 叽叽 jī
小鸭叫 yā 嘎嘎 gā
小羊叫 yáng 咩咩 miē
小牛叫 niú 哞哞 mōu

25

Read and circle the characters that have 扌. Then complete the characters in the boxes.

找 朋 友   握 握 手
摇 摇 头   扭 一 扭
                拍 皮 球

32

Find the hidden 手 in these characters. Some of them may have slight changes.

拳头 拿 攀岩 拜年

30

Find and trace 足 in these characters.

跳绳　踢球　蹦床
走路　踩水坑　跟我来

36

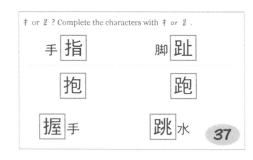

扌 or 足? Complete the characters with 扌 or 足.

手指　　脚趾
抱　　　跑
握手　　跳水

37

Read this nursery rhyme and circle the words with 足.

小白兔，白又白，
两只耳朵 竖起来。
爱吃萝卜和青菜，
蹦蹦跳跳真可爱。

37

Find and trace 目 in these characters.

看书　眉毛　睡觉　照相
眼镜　　睁开眼睛

38

What does a plant need to grow? Circle the words.

40

日光　　　月光
火　　土　　牛奶
　　空气
面包　　　水
　　小鸟

Find and trace 氵 in these characters.

出汗　渴了　果汁
游泳　洗澡　吹泡泡

42

Read and circle the characters that have 氵.

42

河里有小鸭，
小鸭爱洗澡。
海里有大鱼，
大鱼吹泡泡。

Find and trace 氵 in these characters.

果冻　冰淇淋
凉快　冲水

43

Find and trace 火 in these characters.

红绿灯　烤面包　烫
烟花　　蜡烛　　灭火

46

Find and trace 木 in these characters.

黑板　学校　森林
两朵花 一棵树

47

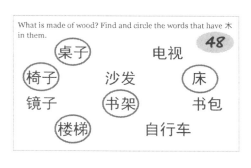

What is made of wood? Find and circle the words that have 木 in them.

48

桌子　　　电视
椅子　　沙发　床
镜子　　书架　书包
楼梯　　自行车

Find and trace 土 in these characters.

地球　灰尘　堆雪人
垃圾　水坑　两块饼干

49

Fill in the boxes with the five elements.

50

火
木　　土
水　　金

Find and trace 日 in these characters.

春节　晚上好　晚安
昨天　明天　晴天

51

Fill in the blanks with 雨/雪.

小雨　中雨　大雨　雨衣
小雪　中雪　大雪　雪人

53

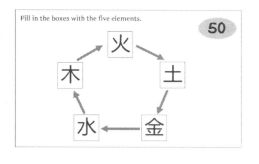

Find and trace 艹 in these characters.

花园　草地　蓝天
白菜　绿茶　萝卜

55

Complete the characters with 艹 and color your favorite fruit!

草莓　　蓝莓
苹果　　葡萄

56

菠萝　　香蕉
芒果　　荔枝

56

Find and trace 宀 in these characters.

小宝宝　客人　晚安
宠物　写字　回家

57

Fill the blanks with the correct 他(们), 她(们), or 它(们).

哥哥在做什么？
他在踢球。

姐姐在做什么？
她在写字。

58

爸爸妈妈在做什么？
他们在骑自行车。

小猫在做什么？
它在捉蝴蝶。

58

Find and trace 饣 in these characters.

米饭　饺子　饿了　饱了

59

Find and trace 米 in these characters.

粥　糖　蛋糕
面粉　奶粉　粉笔

61

它是什么？ What is it? Circle the correct word.

米饭　面包　(蛋糕)　饺子

62

Find and trace 衤/衣 in these characters.

衬衫　裙子　裤子
袖子　毛衣　棉袄

63

Read and circle the characters that have 衤.

妹妹穿短(裙)，姐姐穿长(裙)。
哥哥穿长(裤)。弟弟穿短(裤)。
爸爸穿长(袖)(衬)(衫)，
妈妈穿短(袖)(衬)(衫)。

64

Find and trace 虫 in these characters.

青蛙　龙虾　螃蟹
蜗牛　蜜蜂　蜂蜜

65

Many animals have 虫 in their names. Most of them are insects and reptiles. Find and color 虫 in these words.

蝴蝶　蜻蜓　蚂蚁
蝙蝠　蜘蛛
萤火虫　蚕　蛇

66

Find and trace 鸟 in these characters.

鹦鹉　天鹅　企鹅
鸽子　老鹰　猫头鹰

67

Find and trace 犭 in these characters.

猴子　狼　熊猫　猪
狮子　狐狸　猎人

69

犭, 虫, or 鸟?

70

Say the name of each animal and help them find their group. Draw a line.

虫　犭　鸟

Quiz Time!

72

Match each radical with the correct picture. Draw a line.

亻　日
虫　口
扌　足
目　氵
宀　米
饣　艹

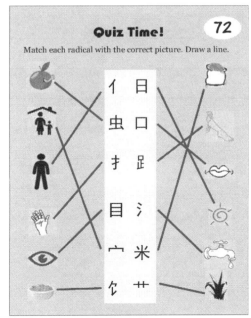

Write the character for each picture. Look at their radicals for hint.

73

	bà			mā
父	爸	女	妈
	máo			jī
犭	猫	鸟	鸡
	dēng			xuě
火	灯	雨	雪
	zuò			wà
土	坐	衤	袜
	bīng			bēi
冫	冰	木	杯

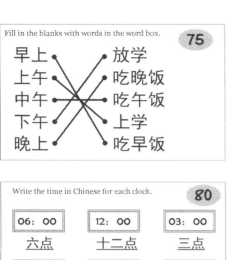

Fill in the blanks with words in the word box. | 75

早上　　放学
上午　　吃晚饭
中午　　吃午饭
下午　　上学
晚上　　吃早饭

Look at the clock and write down the time. | 77

四点　　六点半　　十二点
十点半　　两点半　　八点

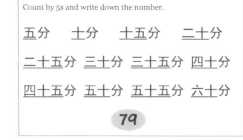

Count by 5s and write down the number. | 79

五分　　十分　　十五分　　二十分
二十五分　　三十分　　三十五分　　四十分
四十五分　　五十分　　五十五分　　六十分

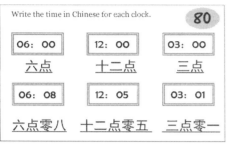

Write the time in Chinese for each clock. | 80

06:00	12:00	03:00
六点	十二点	三点
06:08	12:05	03:01
六点零八	十二点零五	三点零一

08:14	09:19	11:30
八点十四	九点十九	十一点半
04:30	02:47	10:56
四点半	两点四十七	十点五十六

80

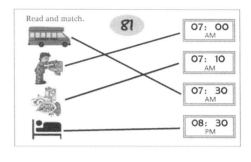

Read and match. | 81

07:00 AM
07:10 AM
07:30 AM
08:30 PM

Circle what you would 穿 and underline what you would 戴 for the activity. | 83

骑自行车　我穿〇，我戴＿＿。

凉鞋　球鞋　拖鞋　皮鞋
手套　帽子　头盔　游泳眼镜

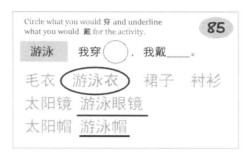

Circle what you would 穿 and underline what you would 戴 for the activity. | 85

游泳　我穿〇，我戴＿＿。

毛衣　游泳衣　裙子　衬衫
太阳镜　游泳眼镜
太阳帽　游泳帽

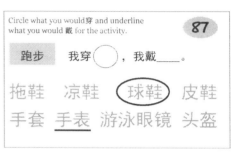

Circle what you would 穿 and underline what you would 戴 for the activity. | 87

跑步　我穿〇，我戴＿＿。

拖鞋　凉鞋　球鞋　皮鞋
手套　手表　游泳眼镜　头盔

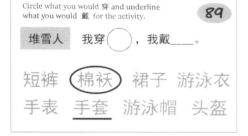

Circle what you would 穿 and underline what you would 戴 for the activity. | 89

堆雪人　我穿〇，我戴＿＿。

短裤　棉袄　裙子　游泳衣
手表　手套　游泳帽　头盔

Look at the pictures and fill in the blanks with words from the word box.

今天天晴。
今天下雨。
今天下雪。
今天天阴。

90

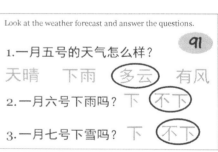

Look at the weather forecast and answer the questions. | 91

1.一月五号的天气怎么样？
天晴　下雨　多云　有风

2.一月六号下雨吗？　下　不下

3.一月七号下雪吗？　下　不下

4.一月八号雨大吗？　大　不大

5.一月九号有风吗？　有　没有

6.一月十号冷吗？　冷　不冷

91

Quiz Time! | 92

Look at each picture and write down the season.

春　夏
冬　秋

Look at each picture and write down the weather. | 93

阴　晴
雨　雪

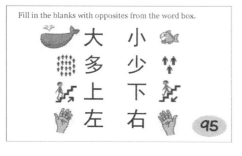

Fill in the blanks with opposites from the word box.

大　小
多　少
上　下
左　右

95

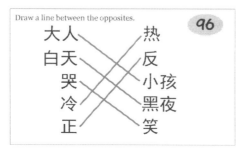

Draw a line between the opposites. | 96

大人　　热
白天　　反
哭　　小孩
冷　　黑夜
正　　笑

Fill in the blanks with opposites from the word box.

好　坏
冬　夏
天　地
早　晚

97

Draw a line between the opposites.

男 — 入
出 — 女
晴 — 雨
主人 — 客人
饿 — 饱

98

姐姐的头发 长 。
弟弟的头发 短 。
猴子的尾巴 长 。
兔子的尾巴 短 。

长裙   短裙
短裤   长裤

长袜   短袜
长袖衬衫   短袖衬衫
长毛狗   短毛狗

100

Fill in the blanks with 高/矮/低.

大人高, 小孩矮。
长颈鹿高，山羊矮。
飞机飞得高，
蜜蜂飞得低。

101

Fill in the blanks with 来/去.

103

妈妈：吃饭了！
明明：来了！
　　爸爸：去不去游泳？
明明：去！

小鱼在水里游来游去。
小鸟在天上飞来飞去。
虫子在地上爬来爬去。

103

Read and draw.
1. 车里有两个人。

104

2. 门外有三棵树。

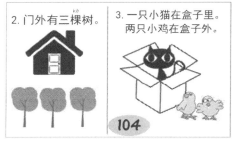

3. 一只小猫在盒子里。
两只小鸡在盒子外。

104

Fill in the blanks with 前/后.

105

长颈鹿在前，大象在后。

Fill in the blanks with opposites from the word box.

大象的鼻子长，猪的鼻子短 。
长颈鹿高，山羊矮。

106 肚子在前，尾巴在后。

Look at the calendar and fill in the date and day of the week for each day.

106

前天	昨天	今天	明天	后天
二月一号	二月二号	二月三号	二月四号	二月五号
星期二	星期三	星期四	星期五	星期六

Read, translate, and answer.

一加一等于几？   1 + 1 = 2
四加七等于几？   4+7=11
十五加九等于几？   15+9=24

109

八减三等于几？   8-3=5
十减六等于几？   10-6=4
十九减二等于几？   19-2=17

109

Radical additions and subtractions. 什么字？

1. 日+月=明
2. 木+不=杯
3. 虫+下=虾
4. 日+十=早
5. 亻+木=休

110

6. 冰-冫=水
7. 们-亻=门
8. 妈-女=马
9. 草-艹=早
10. 字-宀=子

110

Fill in the blanks with 开/关, 打开/关上.

111

开门 ⟷ 关门
开灯 ⟷ 关灯
把门打开 ⟷ 把门关上
把灯打开 ⟷ 把灯关上
把电视打开 ⟷ 把电视关上

Quiz Time!
112
Look, draw, and write the opposites.

⬆ 上   ⬇ 下
⬅ 左   ➡ 右

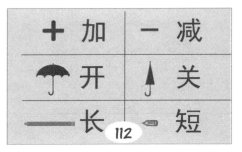

十 加 | 一 减
开 | 关
长   短

112

晴 雨 高 矮 里 外 **113**

好 坏 男 女 **113**

Look, ask, and answer.
1. 谁在看书？ 多多在看书。
2. 谁在扫地？ 爸爸在扫地。
3. 谁爱吃虫子？ 小鸡爱吃虫子。
4. 谁吃了弟弟的蛋糕？
   小猫吃了他的蛋糕。 **115**

Look, read, and match. **116**
谁的鼻子长？
谁的牙齿尖？
谁的尾巴短？
这是谁的袜子？
谁的名字叫多多？
这是谁的脚印？

Fill in the blanks with 什么 and circle the correct answers. **117**
1. 天上有什么？ (太阳)
2. 地里有什么？ (萝卜)
3. 什么动物晚上不睡觉？ (猫头鹰)
4. 什么动物捉老鼠？ (猫)

Read and match.
什么动物叫"喵喵"？   小羊
什么动物叫"咩咩"？   企鹅
什么鸟不会飞？   萤火虫
什么虫会发光？   小猫 **118**

Count the numbers of cows, sheep, and horses that Old McDonald has on his farm.

有六头牛, 五只羊, 两匹马。

119

Answer the questions in Chinese.
1. 等于九。 **120**
2. 等于六。
6. 一年有四个季节。
7. 一个星期有七天。

Complete the questions with 几岁 or 多大.

你妹妹今年几岁？

你爸爸今年多大？

121

Write out the numbers in Chinese.

一块　三块　两块一　七块六
一毛　四毛　两毛五　九毛九
五分　八分　一块九毛九　两块八毛八

122

Look, read, and answer. Use 块/毛. **123**
1. 二十五块。
2. 十九块。
3. 四毛九一磅。
4. 三块八毛九一个。

Find and color these items in the picture. **124**
chuáng   shū bāo   diàn shì
床   书包   电视
bed   backpack   TV

shuǐ bēi   kù zi   qiú xié
水杯   裤子   球鞋
watercup   pants   tennis shoes

Read and match.
1. 哪一个是老师？
2. 哪些是学生？
3. 哪个是医生？
4. 哪个是警察？ **126**
126

哪 (一) 天？ Which day? **126**
1. 十二月二十五号。
2. 一月一号。
怎么了？ What happened? Read and circle.
1. (他摔倒了)
2. (他的牙掉了) **128**

怎么办？ What to do? Read and circle. **129**
1. 戴眼镜 打球 (打伞)
2. 戴手表 (穿棉袄) 穿短裤
3. 找警察 去公园 (看医生)
4. (开灯) 开门 开电视

---

1. 水水 (冰冰) **132**
2. (六岁) 七岁
3. 二年级 (一年级)
4. (中国) 美国
5. 坐校车 (坐公交车)
6. 25 个 (35 个)

也 or 都？ Fill in the blanks.
1. 我爱吃草莓，哥哥也爱吃草莓。
   我们都爱吃草莓。
2. 蜜蜂会飞，蝴蝶也会飞。
   蜜蜂和蝴蝶都会飞。 **138**

3. 今天不下雪，明天也不下雪。
   今天和明天都不下雪。

4. 牛吃草，羊也吃草。
   牛和羊都吃草。 **138**

Fill in the blanks with 用 and match the activities with the correct body parts.

我**用**眼睛 —— 闻花香。
我**用**耳朵 —— 画画。
我**用**鼻子 —— 听音乐。
我**用**嘴巴 —— 跑步。
我**用**手 —— 看书。
我**用**脚 —— 吃东西。

139

Draw a line from each word to the matching face part. Use the word box for hint.

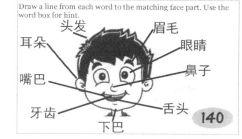

头发　眉毛
耳朵　眼睛
嘴巴　鼻子
牙齿　舌头
下巴

140

Read and write/trace.

从一写到十.　　从 A 写到 G.

一二三四五
六七八九十

ABCDEFG

143

Extend the words with 到 and complete the sentences with the words in the word box.

144

1. 我**看到**天上有星星。
2. 我**听到**树上小鸟叫。
3. 我**闻到**蛋糕的香味。
4. 我**找到**一个好朋友。

一只海狸去旅行 A Beaver Goes on a Trip

Beaver, beaver,
What do you do with your ears?
I listen to sounds with my ears.
What sound do you hear?
I hear the ocean singing a song.

 （ears）听声音

145

Beaver, beaver, 　145
What do you do with your nose?
I smell scents with my nose.
What scent do you smell?
I smell the fragrance of flowers.　（nose）闻气味

Beaver, beaver,
What do you do with your eyes?
I look at things with my eyes.
What thing do you see?
I see some red clouds.　（eyes）看东西

Beaver, beaver,　146
What do you do with your mouth?
I talk with my mouth.
What do you say?
I say, "hello, ocean!"　（mouth）说话

Beaver, beaver,
What do you do with your hands?
I carry things with my hands.
What thing are you carrying?
I am carrying my luggage.　（hands）拿东西

Beaver, beaver,　146
What do you do with your feet?
I walk with my feet.
Where are you walking to?
I'm walking to travel.　（feet）走路

Fill in the blanks with 想 and match the feelings with the desires.

小猫渴了，—— 它**想**睡觉
小猴困了，—— 他**想**吃冰棍
弟弟饿了，—— 它**想**喝水
女孩冷了，—— 他**想**吃饭
男孩热了，—— 她**想**回家

147

Circle all that apply. 妹妹为什么不睡觉？

（她**想**妈妈）
（她**想**爸爸）
（她**想**哥哥）
（她**想**吃冰淇淋）

148

Help the waiter find food for each customer.

我**要**四个饺子。
我**要**一个冰淇淋。
我**要**一杯绿茶。
我**要**两块饼干。
我**要**一杯果汁，不要加冰。

149

Compare and circle the correct words.

151

1. 西瓜比苹果（大）小 。
2. 冬天比夏天 热（冷） 。
3. 女孩比男孩（头发长）头发短 。
4. 长颈鹿比山羊（高）矮 。
5. 多多比云云 大一岁（小一岁） 。

Read, count, and draw.

圆形有三个。　　三角形比圆形多一个。

〇〇〇　　△△△△

蜻蜓飞得低。　　小鸟比蜻蜓飞得高。

152

正方形有五个。　心形比正方形少两个。

□□□
□□

♡♡♡

兔子尾巴短。　　猴子比兔子尾巴长。

152

Quiz Time!

1. 小鸡和小鸭都吃虫子。
2. 他的眼睛是黑色，头发也是黑色。
3. 我会**丛**一写**到**十。
4. 我**用**眼睛看书。

154

5. 长大了，我要去中国。
6. 哥哥比弟弟大三岁。
　 弟弟**没有**哥哥高。
7. 我想和你**做**朋友。

154

Can you find the pattern? Cut, paste, and read.

一人 大，二人 天。

小土 尘，小大 尖。

一火 灭，田力 男。

155

人木 休，手目 看。

人从 众，木林 森。

日月 明，女子 好。

155

Congratulations!

祝贺＿＿＿＿小朋友！

你完成了《小手写中文》

一年级的学习。

特发此证，以资鼓励。

Are you ready for the next level?

Read each character aloud and tell its meaning in English, or say it in a word/sentence in Chinese. As you go along, color in the boxes for the characters you know.

今	伞	妈	爸	爷	听	名	打	找
足	跑	目	眼	看	江	河	冰	冷
灯	灰	杯	朵	地	坐	明	春	星
雨	雪	雷	花	草	它	家	饭	饼
粉	籽	袜	袋	虫	虾	蛋	鸡	鸭
猫	狗	早	午	晚	点	半	分	春
夏	秋	冬	阴	晴	短	高	矮	低
来	去	里	外	前	后	加	减	开
关	谁	什	么	哪	怎	因	为	也
都	用	做	从	到	想	要	比	没

If you've colored 80 or more boxes, congratulations! You may now move on to the next level! If not, don't feel discouraged. Take some time to review this book. Once you are comfortable with the material, take this test again and sure enough, you'll move on!

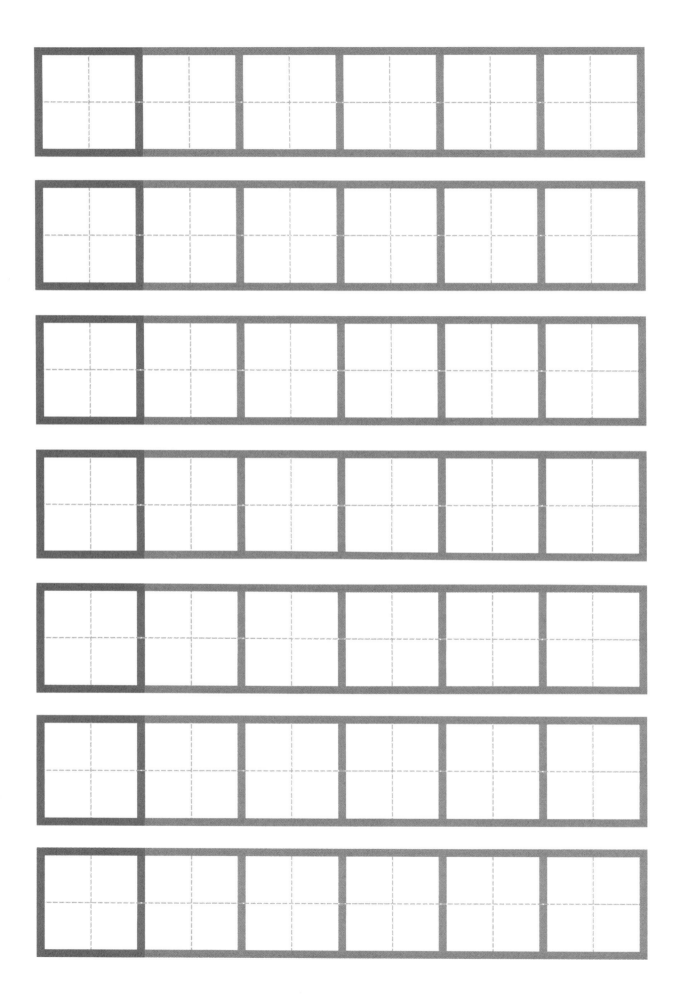

Made in the USA
Columbia, SC
30 May 2017